MICHAEL FARADAY

AND THE
NATURE OF ELECTRICITY

Michael Faraday
and the
Nature of Electricity

Roberta Baxter

MORGAN REYNOLDS

PUBLISHING

Greensboro, North Carolina

the *Profiles*
IN SCIENCE

series includes biographies about . . .

Nikola Tesla
Louis Pasteur
Mary Anning
Lise Meitner
Tycho Brahe
Johannes Kepler
Nicholas Copernicus
Galileo Galilei
Isaac Newton

Robert Boyle
Rosalind Franklin
Ibn al-Haytham
Edmond Halley
Marie Curie
Caroline Herschel
Thomas Edison
Michael Faraday

MICHAEL FARADAY AND THE NATURE OF ELECTRICITY

Copyright © 2009 By Roberta Baxter

Library of Congress Cataloging-in-Publication Data

Baxter, Roberta, 1952-
    Michael Faraday and the nature of electricity / by Roberta Baxter. -- 1st
ed.
        p. cm. -- (Profiles in science)
    Includes bibliographical references and index.
    ISBN-13: 978-1-59935-086-8
    ISBN-10: 1-59935-086-6
    1. Faraday, Michael, 1791-1867. 2. Physicists--Great Britain--Biography. 3.
Chemists--Great Britain--Biography. 4. Electromagnetism. I. Title.
    QC16.F2B39 2008
    530.092--dc22
    [B]
                                        2008018478

Printed in the United States of America
First Edition

To my son, Eric K. Baxter, a computer engineer who counts
Mike Faraday as one of his heroes

Contents

Michael Faraday

one
Blacksmith's Son, Bookbinder's Apprentice

On Monday, August 29, 1831, Michael Faraday started a new section in his laboratory notebook with the heading "Expts. On the production of Electricity from Magnetism, etc. etc." Beginning with the first paragraph, he recorded experiments that changed the world. An iron ring bristling with wires and pieces of twine and paper was connected to a battery. Nearby a compass needle twitched under Faraday's careful eye. When the connection to the battery was broken, another twitch occurred. Faraday had just performed electromagnetic induction—the creation of a force that would change the world.

Michael Faraday was born on September 22, 1791, into a tradesman's family. In 1756, Robert Faraday married Elizabeth Dean, a young woman he had met at church. The church they attended would be not only their meeting place, but the foundation of their lives and of their grandson, Michael. The Faradays lived near Clapham, a village in northwest England on a small farm that had belonged to Elizabeth's father, who had recently died. The small farm, a bobbin mill operated by a stream, and fabrics woven by the women barely provided enough to support the growing family, which grew to include ten children. Richard, the oldest son, moved to Kirkby Stephen, became a prosperous merchant and married a woman he met at the church there. The third son, James, was apprenticed to a blacksmith. Once his apprenticeship was finished, his older brother persuaded him to move to Outhgill, near where Richard lived. Richard's wife had a sister, Margaret, who was working as a maid. James and Margaret took to each other, and were married in June 1786.

For a few years, the family thrived. James Faraday had plenty of blacksmith work to do and children were born to the couple; Elizabeth, in 1787 and Robert, in 1788. However, the French Revolution was causing economic changes in England. A depression occurred, with prices rising, wages falling, and people spending less and less. James began to suffer health problems. He decided to move the family near London in hopes of finding more work there.

In 1791, the family moved to a village on the outskirts of London. Michael Faraday was born there on September 22, 1791. The family moved again in 1796 to living quarters over a coach-house in Jacob's Well Mews, London. Eventually, ten children were born to the family.

James worked as a blacksmith as often as he could, but his fragile health (he probably suffered from rheumatism) continued to plague him. Because of his problems, the family often had little to eat or wear.

For children in the tradesman's class of society, schooling was rare. Michael received only the most rudimentary education. No child from this level of society expected to be able to attend higher schools or dream of a university education.

Michael was unable to correctly pronounce the letter R. For his whole life, he spoke his last name as "Fawaday." One day in school, he mentioned his brother, "Wobert." The schoolteacher gave Robert a halfpenny to buy a cane to thrash Michael until he could speak his Rs. Robert refused, threw the coin away, and told his mother. She immediately took both boys out of the school.

The church that the family attended was a bulwark to their lives. The group was called the Sandemanians, because of the founder Robert Sandeman. A Scotsman, Sandeman, had pulled out of the Anglican Church, the official church of England, Scotland, and Wales. He believed that these churches were corrupt, politically motivated, and not following the teachings of the New Testament. Because of their stand against the official church, Sandemanians were known as dissenters, though their Christian beliefs were not dramatically dissimilar to Anglicans: they believed that God exists and that Christ died for the sins of the world. Their services were simple exercises of singing without instrumental accompaniment, reading of the Bible, the Lord's Supper, and teaching. Guided by the teachings of the church, the Faraday children were taught to obey God, love their fellow church members, and serve their community.

In 1804 at age thirteen, Michael was old enough to earn money to help his family. He convinced a bookbinder and seller, George Riebau, to hire him as a messenger. People who couldn't afford to buy newspapers borrowed from Riebau's shop; one of Michael's first jobs was delivering newspapers to customers and then picking them up later.

Michael demonstrated a sharp mind and strong work ethic, and Riebau decided to accept him as an apprentice. Michael would work and live at the shop for seven years while he was trained in the business of bookbinding. At the end of the training time, Michael would be free to work as a bookbinder in Riebau's or another shop or set up his own bookbinding business. His indenture papers were signed on October 7, 1805. Michael had just turned fourteen years old the month before.

The bookbinder's shop smelled of paper, ink, leather, and glue. Printers would send pages of books to the shop. Michael learned to trim the pages and fold them into sections, called signatures. Michael would stitch the signatures together and pound them down with a mallet so the book was ready for a cover. Michael boasted later that he could strike one thousand times with the mallet before needing to rest. Most of the covers were constructed of leather. Riebau taught him to choose the right section of leather from the hides they had stacked in the yard. The leather was glued to boards for the cover and the signatures of pages were glued inside. A coating of egg white glazed the cover and it was polished with an iron. Finally, the title was stamped in gold and the book was finished.

Michael not only learned to bind the books that passed through the shop. He spent his evening hours reading most of them. Riebau recognized the intelligence of his apprentice and encouraged him in his reading. He even offered books from his own library for his apprentice's learning. So Michael read books ranging from romances to adventures like *Arabian Nights* to reference books.

Three books that entered Riebau's shop changed the direction of Michael's life. Isaac Watts wrote *Improvement of the Mind,* a book that set forth a system to help a man live a wor-

Faraday developed many lifelong habits based on the writings of Isaac Watts. *(Courtesy of Mary Evans Picture Library/Alamy)*

thy life. Watts, a preacher and also the author of the hymn "Joy to the World" among others, listed a multitude of proverbs and advice for any young man to follow. He wrote, "Even the lower orders of men have particular callings in life, wherein they ought to acquire a just degree of skill."

Watts's book inspired Michael to start a program of self-improvement. He took lessons in elocution and instructed friends to correct his speech and spelling when needed. He took drawing lessons from a French refugee living about Riebau's shop.

Two of Watts's precepts struck chords in Michael's mind and he followed them the rest of his life. First, Watts stated that only close observation could discern truth and that speech should always be concise and clear. Second, Watts suggested that a young man should write his observations in a notebook. Michael did so, compiling a book he titled, *The Philosophical Miscellany.* The title page states that the book is "intended to promote both Amusement and Instruction and also to corroborate or invalidate those theories which are continually starting into the world of science." The first few pages show details and drawings taken from articles he read about varying subjects such as boiling tar, filtration, lightning, hair, and formation of snow.

While binding *Encyclopaedia Britannica,* Michael discovered a long article on electricity written by Scottish inventor James Tytler. Tytler stated that all agreed that electricity existed in two types: negative and positive, as named by the American philosopher, Benjamin Franklin. Scientists envisioned electric charge as an imponderable fluid that pulsed through matter, supposedly flowing through without affecting the matter. Another hypothesis was that these fluids

While binding the *Encyclopaedia Britannica*, Michael read about the disagreement between Benjamin Franklin and other scientists about the properties of electricity. *(Library of Congress)*

influenced one another at a distance, a concept that Faraday would someday challenge.

However, scientists disagreed strongly on the rest of the explanation for electricity. French scientists proposed that electricity was really two fluids, one negative and one positive, that flowed in opposite directions. Franklin and most English scientists believed that electricity was one fluid that exhibited negative or positive attributes based on a deficit or surplus of charge. From this *Encyclopaedia Britannica* article, Michael could see the controversy about electricity that existed between scientists.

Another book that Michael devoured was *Conversations in Chemistry,* by Jane Marcet. This book covered chemical experiments, along with theory in clear concise language. One writer said that Marcet, "had so much *accurate* information and who can give it out in narrative so clearly, so much for the pleasure and benefit of others without the least ostentation or mock humility."

In Marcet's opinion, chemistry should be considered not only valuable for the refiner or pharmacist. She said, "the most wonderful and most interesting phenomena of nature are almost all of them produced by chemical powers." Michael later stated that her book "gave me my foundations in that science . . . her book came to me as the full light in my mind."

Reading the books of Watts, the *Encyclopaedia Britannica,* and Marcet gave Michael a glimpse of the scientific world. With his curiosity ignited, he gathered equipment to conduct his own experiments. He bought two jars from a secondhand store and constructed his own equipment for electrical experiments: a electrostatic generator and a Leyden jar.

Jane Marcet *(Courtesy of The Royal Institution/The Bridgeman Art Library)*

An electrostatic generator produces an electric charge through the friction of a piece of leather pressing against the side of a jar as the jar is turned. The static electricity generated is captured by a metal comb or a Leyden jar. Named for the University of Leyden in the Netherlands, where it was invented, a Leyden jar consists of a glass or pottery jar covered with a metal coating. When electricity is generated and fed onto the metal ball at the top of the jar, it flows into the jar and is stored. To release the electrical charge, a metal loop is put into contact with the metal ball and the metallic coating on the side of the jar, causing a spark. Michael constructed these two pieces of equipment and learned how to generate and discharge electrical charges.

Riebau understood the curiosity of his young apprentice. He urged him to attend lectures of the new City Philosophical Society, given in the home of John Tatum. Michael's brother, Robert, gave him the shilling fee for the lectures. Groups of men would meet in the evenings and Tatum or other members would lecture on a variety of scientific subjects, ranging from electricity to chemistry to geology to physics. In one demonstration, Tatum spelled out "SCIENCE" using an electrical spark and a piece of wrinkled silver foil.

Michael began attending these lectures in February 1810. He carried paper stitched as a small book and took notes during the lecture—noting "the most prominent words, short but important sentences, titles of the experiments, names of what substances came under consideration and many other hints that would tend to bring what had passed to my mind." Over the next two nights, he would expand on his original notes and eventually would write out the lecture from his notes,

A sketch of John Tatum's lecture room drawn by Faraday in 1810.
(Courtesy of The Royal Institution/The Bridgeman Art Library)

including drawings of the equipment and even of the room where the lectures were held.

Later, when he bound his notes of the Tatum lectures, Faraday dedicated them to Riebau with these words: "Sir, when I first evinced a predilection for the Sciences . . . you kindly interested yourself in the progress I made . . . Permit me therefore Sir to return thanks in this manner for the many favours I have received at your hands and by your means, and believe me your grateful and Obedient Servant, M Faraday." In the signature under the dedication can be seen the unusual way that Michael began to sign his name. He would write the F first and then M and –araday.

Riebau encouraged Michael to view art at London exhibitions and even from art collections of his customers. He also gave his apprentice time to view mechanical wonders around London; new steam-driven pumps and equipment constructing new highways.

These books, lectures and mechanical sights constituted an education for Michael. But he was about to enter a relationship that would launch him into the scientific world.

two

Scientific Apprentice

With pride in his apprentice's initiative, Riebau showed Faraday's copies and drawings of lecture notes from the City Philosophical Society to George Dance the Younger, as he was called to distinguish him from his father. Dance was an architect (as was his father) responsible for designing numerous buildings in London. Recognizing potential from the notes he saw, Dance gave Faraday tickets to attend four lectures given by Sir Humphry Davy, a famed scientist.

Davy was experimenting with electricity as were many scientists of the time. A huge battery in the basement of the Royal Institution provided power for Davy to conduct all sorts of experiments. By sticking electrodes into solutions and running the power, Davy was able to isolate elemental metals of sodium, potassium, calcium, barium, magnesium,

SIR HUMPHREY DAVY.

Sir Humphry Davy

and strontium. He was the first to find the elemental forms of these atoms.

In his experiments, Davy demonstrated that not all the action took place at the electrodes. The solution in an electrochemical reaction also plays a part. As an example, Davy filled three vessels with solutions and connected them by wicks. One outside beaker held sodium sulfate and the other barium nitrate. The center beaker held water. When electricity was applied to the two outside vessels, a precipitate of barium sulfate appeared in the center vessel, showing that the barium and sulfate had moved into the center by the influence of the electricity.

As England's most famous chemist of the time, Davy was involved in a dispute over Antoine Lavoisier's theory about acids. Lavoisier had set chemistry on a clear and solid path by demolishing the false theory of phlogiston. He proved that combustion and respiration occur by reaction of substances with oxygen. However, he also believed that all acids contain oxygen.

A majority of acids do contain oxygen, but one called muriatic acid refused to be decomposed into oxygen and other

Antoine Lavoisier *(Library of Congress)*

elements. Today we call this strong substance hydrochloric acid. Davy applied electricity to a solution of the acid and only hydrogen and a greenish gas appeared at the electrodes. The greenish gas, Davy called chlorine. Since muriatic acid did not contain oxygen, Lavoisier's theory was wrong.

Many scientists thought that if one part of a theory was wrong, the whole theory was wrong. Even though Lavoisier was wrong about the content of acids, he was right about the action of oxygen in combustion and respiration. French scientists at first refused to accept chlorine as a chemical element. Through experiments, Davy showed it couldn't be broken down further, proving it is an element.

From his experiments, Davy concluded that the reaction of chemicals depends on some innate electrical quality. Because of this quality, some elements always appeared at the negative electrode and others at the positive.

Davy was a member of the Royal Institution of Great Britain. The Royal Institution had been founded in 1799 by fifty-eight men who gave the Institution the mission of promoting education and industrial progress. The Institution never quite reached its intended goal of educating the public as a whole, but it did become an important research center.

When Davy lectured at the Royal Institution, the audience was packed with admirers. Davy would demonstrate an exploding volcano, the effects of breathing nitrous oxide (laughing gas), or experiments with electricity.

When Faraday attended the Davy lectures, he had to sit in the balcony because his social position did not permit him to mingle with the high-class people on the first floor. From his second-floor seat, Faraday listened intently and took copious notes on Davy's experiments. The first lecture that Faraday attended and the sixth one given by Davy was titled "Radiant Matter"—light. During the seminar dated February 29, 1812, Davy explained the sources of light, how reflection and refraction work, and the action of prisms and mirrors.

For one experiment, an assistant used a bellows to ignite charcoal in a pan. Davy tossed some gunpowder into a pan below the one with the charcoal. After a few seconds, the powder exploded. Davy summed up the experiment with, "It is evident that in this experiment the whole of the effect must take place by the radiated heat for none can descend by other means from the pan of coals to the powder."

Faraday sat in his balcony seat above the clock. Throughout the lecture, he wrote notes on a pad spread on the top of his hat, which he perched on his knees. After each lecture, he would spend a couple of evenings writing out full accounts from his notes, including drawings of the lecture hall, equipment used, and the demonstrations performed.

Meanwhile, as Faraday's interest in science was increasing, he was looking for a job. His apprenticeship with Riebau was ending. Faraday appreciated the skills and encouragement he had received in Riebau's shop, but he didn't want to continue as a bookbinder. He wished for a job in science.

He wrote to Sir Joseph Banks, president of the Royal Society, asking for any job, including washing lab dishes. After waiting several days and asking the porter for a reply, an answer was finally given. "The letter requires no answer." In other words, Faraday was not important enough to even reject for a job.

Faraday embarked on a new way to enhance his scientific thoughts. He and a friend, Benjamin Abbott, began

Benjamin Abbott *(Courtesy of The Royal Institution/The Bridgeman Art Library)*

corresponding with each other. They both lived in London, but far enough apart that they didn't see each other daily. In *The Improvement of the Mind*, the book admired by Faraday, Isaac Watts had recommended correspondence as a way to organize and understand ideas. In a letter to Abbott, Faraday concluded that "letter writing improves: first, the hand writing, secondly the—" Here he is stuck for the word, a memory problem that would plague him for his entire life. Then he picks up, "the expression, the delivery, the composition, a manner of connecting words. Thirdly it improves the mind, by the reciprocal exchange of knowledge. Fourthly, the ideas; it tends I conceive to make the ideas clear and distinct . . . Fifthly, it improves the morals."

The young men started corresponding and kept the practice going for several years. They wrote about conversations they had with each other and family members, about their day-to-day experiences, and about experiments. Only the letters written by Faraday were saved, but the tone of the correspondence is clear from those. In one exuberant letter, Faraday recounts a walk in a rainstorm and the ideas that flowed through his mind. "I found myself in the midst of a puddle and quandary of thoughts respecting the heat generated by animal bodies by exercise . . . I proceeded from thence deeply immersed in thoughts respecting the resistance of fluids to bodies precipitated into them." He also made observations on inclined planes, friction, momentum of falling bodies, and cloud types.

In 1800, Alessandro Volta had stacked metal disks together with soaked pieces of cardboard between them and created the first battery. The measure for electrical potential, the volt, is named for him.

Faraday kept up his scientific experiments in Riebau's back room. He built a battery out of copper, felt, and zinc, then a new metal. With his battery, he decomposed Epsom salts—a compound of magnesium sulfate. Then he saved enough to buy more zinc and a piece of copper and built a better battery. As he wrote to Abbott about his experiments, "I found that some of the zinc discs had got a coating . . . of metallic copper, and that some of the copper discs had a coating of the oxide of tin." This observation would later lead him to a theory about how electricity flowed.

The letter writing between Faraday and Abbott continued briskly through the wet summer of 1812. By fall of that year, Faraday's apprenticeship with Riebau was ending. However, Riebau had one more suggestion for the advancement of his apprentice. He persuaded Faraday to bind a copy of the notes he had taken of the Davy lectures and send them to Davy himself.

By the time Faraday sent the lectures to Davy, he was working in another bookbinder shop, for a man named Henry de la Roche. This job was not as pleasant as his apprenticeship with Riebau. De la Roche had a fiery temper, often exercised on his newest employee. While working in de la Roche's shop, there was not time for experiments or evenings with the City Philosophical Society. In a letter to a friend, John Huxtable, Faraday wrote that he wanted to leave "at the first convenient opportunity." He added that "I must resign philosophy [science] to those who are more fortunate in the possession of time and means."

At the time that Faraday sent his lecture notes to Davy, the great scientist had been in Scotland. However, a letter from French scientist, André-Marie Ampère brought Davy back to his laboratory. Ampère had written about a new compound of chlorine and nitrogen that was highly explosive. Because of his discovery of chlorine and his defense of it as an element against French scientists, Davy felt he had to investigate this new compound for himself. He returned to London and began experiments.

Davy combined ammonium nitrate and chlorine in a glass tube and the mixture exploded. Davy's eyes were injured in the explosion. This misfortune completely changed Michael Faraday's life. Unable to read or write because of his accident, he recalled the letter and careful notes he'd received from Faraday, and hired the young man to act as his scribe until his eyes healed. Faraday took on the secretarial work with Davy on top of his duties as bookbinder. The few days he spent with Davy focused Faraday's desire to become a part of the scientific world.

Davy acknowledged Faraday's copy of lecture notes after their time together with a note sent on Christmas Eve. Faraday treasured the note, even though Davy mistakenly wrote his name as Mr. P. Faraday. Davy praised Faraday's "great zeal, power of memory & attention" and says he would like to see him after his return to London in January.

Faraday continued to work as a bookbinder even as de la Roche discouraged his interest in science. De la Roche had no children, so he offered to make Faraday his heir, so that one day he would become a "man of property," a step up from working for others. Faraday declined the proposition, further exacerbating the tension between them.

Davy soon changed Faraday's life. An assistant at the Royal Institution was fired for being involved in a brawl. Davy recommended Faraday as a replacement with a note to the Royal Institution managers that said, "I have found a person who is desirous to occupy the situation . . . His name is Michael Faraday. He is a youth of twenty-two years of age. As far as I have been able to ascertain, he appears well fitted for the situation. His habits seem good, his disposition is active and cheerful, his manner intelligent." The Institution, in turn, offered Faraday the position.

Faraday accepted the offer, with the stipulation that he be provided a laboratory apron and the chance to use the equipment for his own experiments. On March 1, 1813, Faraday began work at the Royal Institution for the pay of twenty-five shillings a week. He also was given rooms in the building for his living quarters.

At the start, Faraday's duties were mostly washing and cleaning lab dishes and equipment. However, soon he was helping Davy with experiments and setting up lecture demonstrations for William Brande, a chemistry professor. In a letter to Abbott, Faraday wrote a long list of ideas about how to conduct a good lecture. He would use these ideas himself in the future.

Davy requested Faraday's assistance with some experiments on nitrogen trichloride, an extremely unstable compound. The men wore glass masks to protect their faces, but during one attempt, Faraday had a tube too close to his face. When it exploded, his mask shattered and part of a fingernail was blown off. He wrote to Abbott, "I have been engaged this afternoon in assisting Sr H in his experiments on it during which we had two or three unexpected explosions."

Life was not all science. Faraday visited his family, attended church services, and met people around London. He played his flute, sang bass with friends, and listened to music from a hotel near his home. With so many interests,

Faraday often wished for more hours in the day. As he wrote Abbott, "What is the longest, and the shortest thing in the world: the swiftest and the most slow: the most divisible and the most extended; the least valued and the most regretted: without which nothing can be done: which devours all that is small: and gives life and spirits to every thing that is great? . . . It is Time."

By this time, Davy had married a wealthy widow and been knighted. He decided to take a long trip to continental Europe, partially for sightseeing and partially for meeting with scientists of other countries. Most Englishmen would not have dared to travel in France at the time because of tensions between the two countries. Napoleon was in power in France and had been in a conflict with England for nearly fifteen years. However, Napoleon and the Institut de France had recognized Davy's work with electrochemistry, awarding him a special medal. So, Napoleon granted a passport for Davy and any who traveled with him. Davy's valet backed out of the trip at the last moment because of his fears of travel in France. Davy asked Faraday to come along as his assistant and valet until a suitable valet could be found in Paris. Faraday hesitated at first, but decided that the trip was the chance of a lifetime.

So began another part of Faraday's education. Most wealthy young men of the time considered their education complete once they had taken The Grand Tour of Europe. Faraday would be taking his Grand Tour with one of the greatest scientists of the time.

Faraday packed Davy's portable laboratory, prepared his employer's clothes, and soon perched on the roof of the carriage as they headed to an English port for passage across the English Channel. Faraday began a journal of the trip.

The group sailed from Plymouth on October 17, 1813. Once they reached Paris, Faraday was insulted and spit upon because of his obvious English clothes. With Davy's advice, he bought French clothes and determined that he must learn the language to fit in better. He admired the architecture of the buildings, gardens, and museums, but did not care for the people, writing to Abbott that "their attentions are to gain money."

As they traveled, Davy and Faraday met with scientists and conducted experiments using the portable laboratory. French chemists told Davy of a violet vapor that was obtained from ashes of seaweed. Chemist Louis Gay-Lussac had called the substance "iode" from the word for violet, but the French had been unable to determine exactly what it was. By experiments, Davy concluded that it was a new element with characteristics similar to the chlorine that he had discovered. He renamed it "iodine." As Faraday wrote, "Davy . . . goes on discovering."

In December, Faraday caught a glimpse of Napoleon riding in his carriage in a procession. He wrote that the distance made it hard to distinguish Napoleon's face, but "he seemed of a dark countenance and somewhat corpulent."

One big disadvantage of traveling with Davy was his wife. Lady Jane Davy strongly believed in the height of her position and the lowliness of maid and valet. She forced Faraday to eat at the servants table in the kitchen and insulted him when Sir Davy was not around. Faraday resented the treatment, but his youth and inexperience kept him quiet. He avoided Lady Davy as much as possible.

Louis Gay-Lussac *(Library of Congress)*

After leaving Paris, the Davys and Faraday spent two months at the Mediterranean coast and then headed across the Alps into Italy. Faraday and Davy walked beside the carriage through the deep snow. Faraday wore a second coat and a night-cap to keep warm, but he also consulted a barometer to determine elevation as they climbed. Finally, they reached Italy.

Crossing the Gulf of Genoa in a boat during a storm, Lady Davy became faint enough to stop speaking. Faraday wrote to Abbott that her silence was worth the risk to their lives.

While in Italy, Faraday and Davy met scientists and saw Galileo's telescope. The Grand Duke of Tuscany allowed Davy to borrow an immense burning glass to conduct an experiment with diamonds.

Scientists knew that diamonds were made of carbon; so is the soot in a fireplace. What was not understood was how carbon could exist in such different forms. Under the strong heat of the burning glass, diamonds evaporated in a few hours. Davy was able to analyze the vapor released and found only carbon dioxide, proving that the diamond was composed only of carbon. The oxygen came from the air.

As they passed through Milan, Faraday was privileged to meet Alessandro Volta, the father of the battery.

With his English sense of superiority, Faraday admired the sights of Rome, but again did not enjoy the people, stating that the civilization had stepped back from its earlier glory to "only a degenerate idle people."

After trips to Naples and the volcano Vesuvius, the group stayed several months at Lake Geneva, Switzerland. Here again Davy and Faraday conferred with scientists. One Swiss scientist commented, "We admired Davy, we loved Faraday."

Faraday was ecstatic when he and the Davys were invited to a dinner party at the home of Jane Marcet, the author of *Conservations in Chemistry*. Lady Davy, however, ordered Faraday to the kitchen with the servants for his meal. After the meal was over, as was the custom, the ladies withdrew to a parlor and Marcet's husband whispered to the men, "And now, my dear Sirs, let us go and join Mr. Faraday in the kitchen."

In a later letter to Abbott, Faraday described Lady Davy. "She is haughty and proud to an excessive degree and delights

Faraday was able to meet Alessandro Volta, inventor of the battery, while traveling through Italy with Davy.

in making her inferiors feel her power." He wondered if the knowledge obtained on the trip had been worth the exposure to Lady Davy.

By early 1815, Faraday was tired of traveling and anxious to return to England. However, the Davys planned to travel to Greece and Turkey, extending the trip for several months. Events intervened to change Sir Davy's plans. Napoleon had been imprisoned on Elba, but escaped, heightening the tension in Europe. Plague also was breaking out, so Davy decided it was time to return to England.

three
Early Experiments at the Royal Institution

The war atmosphere that sent Davy and Faraday home from Europe ended with the report of the Duke of Wellington's victory over Napoleon at Waterloo. As London celebrated, Faraday continued his scientific work at the Royal Institution and his leisure time activities with the City Philosophical Society.

After his return to England, Faraday returned to work at the Royal Institution. On the recommendation of Davy, he was given a raise and title: assistant and superintendent of the Apparatus and Mineralogical Collection. The title proclaimed his rise from bottle washer to scientist, though a junior one. He began to move out of his time as scientific apprentice and into full membership in the scientific community.

Sir Humphry Davy continued to travel extensively. He would turn up at the Royal Institution for a few days and then be off on an excursion to Scotland or Wales. Faraday's duties included analyzing samples sent in from Davy's travels. Vials of air from coal mines or ore samples would arrive at the Royal Institution for Faraday to examine. Davy praised Faraday's experimental expertise in one letter. Asking Faraday to analyze a supposed new acid discovered by Irish chemist, Michael Donovan, Davy writes "Pray make an investigation of this subject. I think you are a better chemist than Donovan." Faraday also had jobs to do for his immediate boss, Professor William Brande. He conducted analyses, set up lectures, and helped compile part of the *Quarterly Journal of Science,* published by the Institution. In his *Manual of Chemistry,* Brande

William Brande

acknowledged Faraday's contribution by writing, "I have uniformly received the active and able assistance of Mr. M. Faraday, whose accuracy and skill as an operator have proved an essential service in all my proceedings."

During this time, Faraday assisted Davy with one of Davy's most well-known inventions, the safety lamp. As England became more industrialized, coal was needed in increasing quantities. British coal mines had suffered numerous casualties due to explosions in mines. The open flames used to light the dark recesses would ignite gases in the mine. To test for possible explosive gas, a miner would wrap himself in wet cloths and creep forward holding a candle ahead of him on a stick. Exploding the gas in this way was dangerous to everyone and didn't guarantee that all the gas had been eliminated. A committee of concerned citizens called on Sir Davy as a famous scientist to find an alternative.

A number of mining safety lamps designed by Davy *(Library of Congress)*

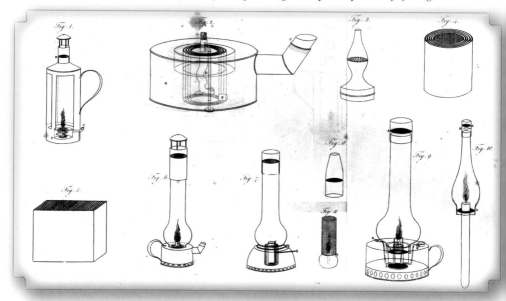

With Faraday's help, Davy determined that the exploding gas was methane and that it only exploded when sufficient levels of oxygen were present. The solution was a wire mesh that absorbed oxygen and dissipated heat set in a framework around a flame. By lowering the concentration of oxygen around the flame, the risk of explosion decreased dramatically. The absorption of oxygen also caused the mesh to glow; the redder the glow, the higher the concentration of methane. Miners used this quality as a guide to safety, evacuating the tunnels when the concentration of methane was high, showing an increased chance of an explosion.

Faraday's contribution to the development of the device was ignored as it became known as the Davy lamp. Davy entered several mine tunnels to instruct miners on the proper use of the lamp. After testing it, the chief engineer of one coal mine stated, "We have subdued this monster."

After the completion of the lamp, Davy returned to his travels, and Faraday again focused on analyzing samples sent to the institution. Faraday's first published paper was the result of a sample of caustic lime sent by Davy from Tuscany. Faraday later added this first paper to a book he wrote, saying "It was the beginning of my communications to the public, and its results very important to me. Sir Humphry Davy gave me the analysis to make as a first attempt in chemistry at a time when my fear was greater than my confidence, and both far greater than my knowledge."

Faraday's days were filled with analyses from others besides Davy. He disproved the existence of a new metal, as claimed by a Viennese scientist. After careful experiments, Faraday concluded that the supposed new metal was actually a mixture of several metals.

Faraday working in his lab at the Royal Institution *(Courtesy of The Royal Institution/The Bridgeman Art Library)*

He worked with compounds of chlorine and carbon, synthesizing a chemical now known as carbon tetrachloride. The molecule is a central carbon with four chlorines attached, and was used extensively in dry cleaning and as an industrial solvent (though today it is known to be a possible carcinogen).

James Stodart, another member of the Royal Institution, requested Faraday's help in an investigation of alloys of steel, searching for a good material for surgical instruments. Their work on iron, steel, and other metals reminded Faraday of his father's blacksmith shop. Over five years, they improved the quality of steel they were able to make.

Most of Faraday's experimental work was impeccable, but in 1819, he made some errors. Davy requested an investigation of phosphorus compounds, repeating some experiments reported by Jons Jacob Berzelius, a Swedish chemist. Faraday's results differed from those of Berzelius and when these were reported, Berzelius published a stinging retort against Davy and Faraday in a chemistry journal. He wrote "If M. Davy would be so kind as to take the pains of repeating these experiments himself he should be convinced of the fact that when it comes to exact analyses, one should never entrust them into the care of another person; and this is above all a necessary rule to observe when it comes to refuting the works of other chemists who have not shown themselves ignorant of the art of making exact experiments."

Faraday did not mention the public criticism in his journal, but he never again allowed publication of his experiments without validation of each result. In later years, other scientists might disagree with Faraday's conclusions but not with his experiments.

In spite of this mistake, Faraday was bombarded with requests for analyses both for government and for private businesses. He analyzed wine, paper, rust, and clay from different parts of the country. The Admiralty, responsible for all things related to the British Navy, requested research on methods of drying meat and fish, and analyses on military oatmeal. Faraday found that some oatmeal was contaminated with chalk to increase the profit of those selling it to the Navy.

1821 Sept 3.

9

Magnetic poles on the outside of the circle the more described

the N pole being perpendicular to the circle

The effect of the wire is always to pass off at a right angle from the pole... tended to go in a circle round it... when either pole was brought up to the wire perpendicular to it & to the radius of the circle it described there was neither attraction nor repulsion but the moment the pole moved in the slightest manner either in or out the wire moved one way or the other

The poles of the magnet act on the bent wire in all positions and not in the direction only of any axis of the magnet so that the current can hardly be cylindrical or around the axis of any kind?

From the motion above a single magnetic pole in the centre of one of the circles should make the wire

A page from Faraday's notebook that describes a "Rotation of Current Experiment" on September 3, 1821.

One assignment was for an insurance company. A sugar refining company had changed the oils used in the manufacturing process. Following a fire at the factory, the insurance company claimed that the new oils caused the destruction, so they were not liable to pay the insurance money. Faraday was recruited to speak as an expert for the insurance company. To his dismay, Davy and Brande were witnesses for the sugar refiner. However, they relied on theory, while Faraday had performed experiments with the volatile oil. His arguments were strong, but the court ordered the insurer to pay the amount of the policy because the refiner had not planned to defraud the insurance company.

Faraday began a series of lectures for the City Philosophical Society (CPS). Starting on January 17, 1816, and continuing through a total of seventeen lectures given over two years, he taught principles of chemistry. His first lecture covered the properties of matter, and others ranged from chemical attractions to heat and combustion. Then he continued into descriptions of specific elements, including chlorine, oxygen, metals, and the alkaline earths. For each lecture, Faraday carefully wrote out his lecture notes and performed demonstrations to illustrate his points.

An anonymous poet at the CPS wrote a poem describing a meeting of the organization, including many of the members. For the part about Faraday, it reads:

> His powers, unshackled, range from pole to pole;
> His mind from error free, from guilt his soul.
> Warmth in his heart, good humor in his face,
> A friend to mirth, but foe to vile grimace;
> A temper candid, manners unassuming,
> Always correct, yet always unassuming.

> Such was the youth, the chief of all the band;
> His name well know, Sir Humphry's right hand.
> With manly ease toward the chair he bends,
> With Watt's Logic at his finger-ends

In April 1819, Faraday recounted his weekly schedule in a letter to Benjamin Abbott. Days were filled with work and then evenings were as follows:

> On Monday evening there is a scientific meeting of Members here [Royal Institution] and every other Monday a dinner, to both of which my company is requested. On Tuesday evening I have a Pupil who comes at 6 o'clk and stops till 9, engaged in private lessons. On Wednesday the [City Philosophical] Society requires my aid. Thursday is my only evening for accidental engagements. Friday, my pupil returns and stops his three hours; and on Saturday I have to arrange my little private business.

Sundays were time for worship with his Sandemanian brothers.

Faraday, with his curly brown hair and round face, was often mistaken for a younger person than he was. But he was at the age to begin to consider romance and marriage. However, he seems to detest the idea. In his *Common Place Book,* which he used as a journal and collection of thoughts and things he read, he wrote a poem, part of which read: "What is the pest and plague of human life? / And what the curse that often brings a wife? / 'tis Love." The poem continues for thirty-five more lines.

One of Faraday's friends, Edward Barnard, was the son of an elder of the Sandemanian church. Edward showed Faraday's poem to his sister, Sarah. After the two met, Faraday became determined to court Sarah and marry her.

He wrote passionate letters to Sarah. After one, which Sarah showed to her parents, they sent Sarah to Ramsgate to visit her sister. Faraday followed her there and tried to attract her love. At first, Sarah did not respond to his presence. In his journal, he wrote, "I wished for a moment that memory and sensation would leave me, and that I could pass away into nothing." He took her on a walk to a windmill and showed her the machinery, but she wasn't interested. Finally, on a trip to Dover, looking across the "brilliant sparkling ocean, stirred with life by a fresh and refreshing wind, and illuminated by a sun which made the waters themselves seem inflamed," Sarah agreed to Faraday's courtship.

Because their church was not the official church of the country, they could not be married there. Only Anglican churches could perform marriages, so Michael Faraday and Sarah were married on June 12, 1821, at St. Augustine's church. By their wishes, the day was not a big celebration. Faraday had written to Sarah's sister, "There will be no bustle, no noise, no hurry occasioned even in one day's proceedings. In externals, the day will pass like all others, for it is in the heart that we expect and look for pleasure." At the time of their marriage, Sarah was twenty-one and Faraday almost thirty.

John Tyndall, years later, noticed a journal entry written by Faraday. It is in third person and says, "On June 12, 1821, he married, an event which more than any other contributed to his earthly happiness and healthful state of mind. The union has continued for twenty-eight years and has in no wise changed, except in the depth and strength of its character."

The couple moved into an apartment on the second floor of the Royal Institution building. Faraday worked below and returned home for a cup of tea when he wished. In a letter written when Sarah was away, Faraday said,

> Oh, my dear Sarah, poets may strive to describe and artists to delineate the happiness which is felt by two hearts truly and mutually loving each other; but it is beyond their efforts, and beyond the thoughts and conceptions of anyone who has not felt it. I have felt it and do feel it, but neither I nor any other man can describe it; nor is it necessary. We are happy, and our God has blessed us with a thousand causes why we should be so.

About a month after they were married, Faraday made his confession of faith before the church, becoming a full member of the Sandemanian fellowship. When Sarah asked him why she had not known he was planning to do so, he replied, "That is between me and my God."

Faraday's Bible, now part of the collection of the Royal Institution, indicates his devoted study. Symbols in the margin indicate scriptures used by different elders in their lessons. The verses found in Job 28:1-2 are underlined: "Surely there is a vein of silver, and a place for gold where they fine it. Iron is taken out of the earth, and brass is molten out of the stone." Also marked are the places where the name Michael is mentioned, for example, Daniel 12:1.

Faraday and Sarah never had any children, but they treasured their nieces and other family members. Years later, one niece remembered, "What a treat a visit to the Laboratory used to be!" Sometimes, to delight his young visitors, Faraday would toss a sliver of potassium into water, causing a brilliant flame. At other times, animals provided the entertainment. After watching tadpoles turn into frogs over several days, some of the mature frogs were missing, free somewhere in the living quarters or the Royal Institution. The rest were turned loose in a nearby park. Another amazing creature remembered by niece Constance Reid was planaria; these animals are able to regenerate parts of their bodies. She wrote, "Cut them in two, each part became perfect."

Faraday enjoyed jokes, puns, and word games. Many examples are found in his *Common Place Book*. One favorite was anagrams—a puzzle where letters from a word or phrase are rearranged into another word or phrase related to the first. Some examples that Faraday recorded:

> O Poison Pit -----Opposition
> Telegraph -----Great help
> No more stars -----Astronomers
> Old England ----golden land
> Radical Reform ----Rare Mad Frolic
> Monarch ----march on

Two more sentences in Faraday's *Common Place Book* are palindromes: sentences that have the same letters backwards and forwards:

> Evil is a name of foeman as I live.
> Madam is an Eve even as I'm Adam.

Sarah did not understand the science of Faraday's work, but she provided him a calm and serene home to relax. The perfect synergy of his work and his home life was marred by one thing: memory problems and headaches. Through his whole life, Faraday struggled with these symptoms. While on an extended vacation, he wrote to a friend, "I am very much better for the country etc. and think I begin to feel as usual; all

I am annoyed about are the nervous headaches and weakness. They unsettle me and make me indisposed to do anything but they are very much better than they were."

With his work and his marriage, Faraday was a happy man. But an observation by a Danish scientist was about to change his world.

four
Experiments and Rotations

O n October 1, 1820, Sir Humphry Davy rushed into the lab with news that would change Faraday's research and eventually, the world. Danish scientist, Hans Christian Ørsted had noticed something new during a demonstration for a science class. When electricity was flowing in a wire, the needle of a nearby compass jumped as the compass was moved closer to the wire. When Ørsted pulled the compass away, the needle jumped in the opposite direction. Compasses are tiny magnets that align with the magnetic field of the earth unless another magnetic force is nearby. Ørsted hypothesized that a magnetic field was generated by the electricity and moved in circles around the wire.

This new phenomena was a curiosity to Davy and Faraday and they began to reenact the experiments, when time was

Hans Christian Ørsted hypothesized that a magnetic field was generated by electricity.

available from Faraday's other duties. For years, scientists had guessed that electricity and magnetism might be the same force, but no one had been able to prove it. Under the laws of nature expounded by Sir Isaac Newton, attraction and repulsion existed between bodies, but always in direct lines. This principal did not seem to hold true with electricity and magnetism. The dependence on Newtonian principles may have blinded other scientists to the circular motion. It was up to Faraday to make the lines of force clear.

André-Marie Ampère, one of the scientists that Faraday had met in Paris, had shown that two wires carrying current in the same direction were attracted to each other and wires with current running in opposite directions were repulsed. He believed that magnetism was the result of two electrical forces, and he postulated that the source of electricity was in the molecules themselves. However, in permanent magnets, no sign of electricity could be found. So while Ampère greatly advanced the science of electricity, his explanation did not hold true with respect to magnetism. (Still the unit for the measuring of an electric current is named for him: the ampere, shortened to amp.)

Ampère presented a mathematical proof of his hypothesis. The mathematics were too much for Faraday's limited education, but what he did understand was not fulfilled by experimentation. After his own experiments and discovery, Faraday wrote to Ampère in 1822,

> I am naturally skeptical in the matter of theories and therefore you must not be angry with me for not admitting the one you have advanced immediately. Its ingenuity and applications are astonishing and exact but I cannot comprehend how the currents are produced and particularly if they be supposed to exist round each atom or particle and I wait for further proofs of their existence before I finally admit them.

The two scientists continued their correspondence for years, and Ampère became one of Faraday's strongest supporters in the storm that was about to break.

William Wollaston, a friend and fellow scientist of Davy, was also intrigued by Ørsted's discovery. He and Davy repeated the experiment reported by Ørsted and others. Wollaston came to the conclusion that current traveled down a wire in a helix fashion and this created a circular magnetic force around the wire, much like closing a fist around the wire. He guessed that a wire carrying current ought to roll in the vicinity of a magnet. Wollaston and Davy tried to produce this effect, but their experiments were not effective. Faraday was probably not present during the experiments because of other duties, but he joined in some of the discussions about electricity and magnetism.

Soon after Ørsted's announcement, Faraday was assigned a chore for the journal of the Royal Institution, *Annals of Philosophy*. He was supposed to review all scientific litera-ture about electricity and write a history of the phenomenon. Faraday not only read all reports about electricity; he dupli-cated the experiments reported by other scientists. The idea developed in his mind that Wollaston was not quite right about a wire rolling in the presence of a magnet. Faraday believed the circular force proposed by Ørsted would cause a wire to revolve around a fixed magnet, much as the moon circles the earth. How could this phenomenon be demonstrated?

After visualizing the effect in his head, Faraday designed an apparatus to demonstrate his thoughts. Sarah's fourteen-year-old brother, George Barnard, was on hand for the experi-ment. On September 3, 1821, Faraday poured mercury, a liquid metal that conducts electricity, into two bowls. Wires descended from a central stand into both bowls. In one bowl, he glued a magnet in an upright position in the mercury. From the stand, a wire was attached with a pivot, allowing it to

William Wollaston *(Courtesy of Classic Image/Alamy)*

rotate freely. The other bowl had a stationary wire plunged into the mercury and a magnet was free to rotate.

When current from a battery was applied to the wires, the demonstration began. In the bowl with the upright magnet, the wire rotated around the magnet. In the other bowl, the magnet revolved around the wire. "There they go! There they go! We have succeeded at last!" Faraday exclaimed. George later remembered, "I shall never forget the enthusiasm expressed in his face and the sparkling in his eyes." In his laboratory notebook, Faraday merely wrote, "Very satisfactory, but make a more sensible apparatus." However, he felt that he and George deserved a treat after the great success, so they took off to go to the circus.

Other scientists had discussed and probably visualized electromagnetic rotation, but Faraday was the first to construct an apparatus showing the phenomenon. Faraday made miniature specimens of his rotator and sent them to scientists around Europe. The first part of his review article about electricity was published in *Annals of Philosophy*, but to keep from appearing to be an expert in the field, Faraday signed the article with the initial M. In October 1821, his article "On some new Electro-Magnetical Motions, and on the Theory of Magnetism" came out in the *Quarterly Journal of Science.* Immediately, a storm of criticism broke out.

Faraday had not acknowledged Wollaston's experiments and thoughts about rotation, and he neglected to mention his scientific mentor, Davy. Faraday was accused of plagiarism.

The storm injured Faraday's pride in his accomplishment. He wrote to his friend, James Stodart, that the words he only heard as whispers were probably talked about among scientists and "as they in part affect my honour and honesty I am anxious to do away with or at least prove erroneous in those parts which are dishonourable to me." In his diary, Faraday had written that he had tried to talk to Wollaston about the rotation experiment, but he was out of town. "I have regretted ever since I did not delay the publication, that I might have shown it first to Dr. Wollaston." But Faraday had not stolen Wollaston's idea. He had improved on it and devised a method to demonstrate the rotation. Faraday wrote Wollaston:

> I am bold enough sir to beg the favour of a few minutes conversation with you on this subject simply for these reasons that I can clear myself satisfactorily—that I owe obligations to you –that I respect you—that I am anxious to escape from unfounded impressions against me—and if I have done any wrong that I may apologise for it.

Wollaston finally did meet with Faraday at the Royal Institution. He did not stir up criticism against Faraday, but he did nothing to exonerate him either. Faraday was on his own in this fight.

Unfortunately, others were not willing to leave the matter alone. Henry Warburton, member of the Royal Society and friend of Wollaston, conducted a campaign against Faraday among his fellow members. The whispers and accusations were bad enough, but then Faraday's mentor, Sir Humphry Davy, entered the fray.

In a speech to the Royal Society in March 1823, Davy stated that Wollaston had attempted electromagnetic rotation before Faraday and that the experiment had only failed because of the equipment. In other words, if the equipment had worked, Wollaston would "have been the discoverer of the phenomenon," according to Davy. When Faraday objected to

Davy's hint that he had stolen the idea from Wollaston, Davy remarked that his statement had been falsely quoted. This incident flamed the issue of plagiarism again.

Davy continued to see Faraday as his servant. In the same months after Faraday discovered electromagnetic rotation, he received orders from Davy while he was on a trip: to send him some dead flies for a fishing lure, to ask his housekeeper to prepare a bed for his brother, and to tell his servants to put down a carpet in his bedroom. This belittling view of Faraday made Davy not willing to acknowledge him as a scientist equal in ability to himself.

Some English friends continued to support Faraday. Richard Phillips published the second part of Faraday's review article, "Historical Sketches of Electro-Magnetism" in *Annals of Philosophy*. Phillips added his own comment at the end of the article: "we earnestly recommend [Faraday] to continue his researches on a subject which he has so ably illustrated and enriched by his discoveries that are in the highest degree curious and important."

Scientists from other countries also praised Faraday's discovery; however, despite the support, the controversy was dragging him down. He wrote to Ampère, "Considering the very subordinate position I hold here and the little encouragement which circumstances hold out to me I have been more than once tempted to resign scientific pursuits altogether."

Faraday's electromagnetic rotation apparatus or dynamo caused a storm of controversy, but today his concept can be seen in many places, including the electric motor. A motor has a permanent magnet and a coil of wire placed between the north and south poles. When current runs through the wire, the interacting fields of the magnet and the current cause the coil to rotate. The commutator switches the direction of the current each half turn, so the poles will continue to repel and the coil will keep spinning. Attach other parts to the axle running through the coil and an electric motor is created that could run in DVD or CD players, a hairdryer, an electric screwdriver, or a computer.

The problem of Sir Davy's criticism and jealousy would haunt Faraday again, but in the meantime, he was busy with other experiments, including one suggested by Davy.

In experiments with alloys conducted by Faraday and Stodart, they often found a film of silver formed on the top of the crucible. This curious effect captured Faraday's attention. He mentioned it in a letter to professor de la Rive in Geneva, saying "I have no doubt at present on the volatility of silver though I had before." Further experiments showed that even a metal like silver can be vaporized. As the vapor cools, it settles on the crucible and becomes solid silver again.

After the silver experiments, Faraday began to wonder if the changes from gas to liquid to solid and back again depended on more than chemical attraction. He hung a piece of gold over some mercury and placed the bottle in a dark place. After some time had passed, he found that the piece of gold was covered with mercury vapors. These experiments led to the suspicion that all substances could be turned into vapor under the right conditions.

Could the opposite change also occur? Can a substance only known as a gas form a liquid or a solid? At the Davy lectures that Faraday had attended in 1812, he heard Davy say, "In solids the matter exerts its attractive powers and remains fixed. In fluids there is an equilibrium between the attractive and repulsive powers. In Gasses the repulsive power preponderates over the Attractive." In other words, physical phases are accounted for by the attraction and repulsion of particles of matter.

Faraday had already discovered compounds of chlorine. He said that chlorine was a favorite topic, so he decided to try to liquefy chlorine gas. In between his duties as assistant to Professor Brande and requests by Davy, he investigated what many considered solid chlorine. Davy had shown that the material was actually a compound of chlorine and water, what would today be called chlorine hydrate.

After analyzing the compound, Faraday agreed that it was a combination of chlorine and water. But his attempts to liquefy chlorine out of the compound failed. When Davy stopped by the laboratory for a short visit, he suggested that Faraday might heat the compound under pressure and see what happened.

As he conducted the experiments, the glass tubes often exploded under the pressure. Sarah would pick the shards of glass out of his skin and at one time, out of his eyes, and he would continue the experiments. As he wrote to a friend, "I met with another explosion on Saturday evening, which has laid up my eyes. It was from one of my tubes, and was so powerful as to drive the pieces of glass like pistol-shot through a window. However I am getting better, and expect to see as well as ever in a few days. My eyes were filled with glass at first."

Faraday described his progress in a paper read to the Royal Society in March, 1823. The sealed tube of compound was placed in water heated at 60° with no change. But when put into water at 100°, changes occurred. "The tube became filled with a bright yellow atmosphere, and on examination was

Faraday (left) poses with an unidentified man during his experiment to liquefy chlorine. *(Courtesy of Hulton Archive/Getty Images)*

found to contain two fluid substances; the one, about three fourths of the whole, was of a faint yellow color, having very much the appearance of water; the remaining fourth was a heavy bright yellow fluid, lying at the bottom of the former, without any apparent tendency to mix with it."

Dr. Paris, a professor at the Royal Institution, saw the results of the experiment and rebuked Faraday for using a dirty tube and contaminating the experiment. After careful analysis that proved that the oily bottom liquid was not a contaminant of chlorine, Faraday sent Paris a note the next day: "Dear Sir, The *oil* you noticed yesterday turns out to be liquid chlorine. Yours faithfully, M. Faraday."

Soon after, Faraday learned that Thomas Northmore had liquefied chlorine in 1805, so he withdrew his claim of being the first to do so.

This time, Faraday carefully acknowledged Davy's suggestion of trying to heat a chlorine compound under pressure. Davy took it a step further, adding a note to the published paper saying that he had foreseen the results that Faraday would have. Faraday felt slighted by this note because Davy only made the suggestion, while Faraday had performed the experiments, including surviving explosions. Davy took credit for a few words, while Faraday had actually done the work.

This controversy came at the same time that another was forming. The premiere scientific establishment in England was not the Royal Institution, but the Royal Society. The Society operated as an exclusive club of the best scientists in the country. Many scientists were members of both the Royal Institution and the Royal Society.

In May, 1823, Richard Phillips told Faraday that he had nominated him to be a Fellow of the Royal Society. About

Faraday in his lab in 1833 *(Courtesy of Mansell/Time Life Pictures/Getty Images)*

twenty-four members, including Wollaston, had signed the nomination certificate. One hold out was the president of the Royal Society, Sir Humphry Davy. At the bottom of the letter telling him of the nomination, Faraday wrote, "Sir H. Davy angry, May 30th."

Davy and a few others campaigned against Faraday's nomination much longer than most people were discussed for membership. Finally, on January 8, 1824, Faraday was elected into the Society with only one dissenting vote. Since the vote was secret, no one knows who cast the nay vote.

In 1825, Davy supported Faraday's promotion to director of the laboratory at the Royal Institution. Soon after, Davy developed a disabling illness and resigned from both institutions. He died in Geneva in 1829.

Now Faraday was a Fellow of the Royal Society, but his main laboratory, the Royal Institution, was in danger of closing. He set to work to save it.

five

Lectures

*T*he Royal Institution, where Faraday worked and lived was in dire financial circumstances. Less money was coming in than what was needed to pay the bills. Lecturers such as William Brande had taken pay cuts, and the 1816 bill for coal (used for heat and for laboratory furnaces) was paid two years late. Faraday's research and analyses for industry provided some money. In 1823, members provided a loan to the Institution, but more funds were needed immediately or the Institution would have to close.

In a letter to Captain John Franklin, who was on a voyage exploring the Arctic, Faraday admitted "we are having a hard struggle to restore the Institution and I have no doubt you will find it when you return in a very different state to that you left it in."

Faraday developed a plan to reach out to the members and the public. In 1826, he began inviting members of the

Faraday corresponded with John Franklin, an Artic explorer, during his efforts to save the Royal Institution from financial ruin.

Institution into the laboratory for talks about recent science happenings. These Friday evening gatherings became so popular that by April 1827, the events were moved to the large lecture hall. Faraday knew that his speaking did not have the flamboyant, poetic style of Sir Humphry Davy, but his clear language and evident wonder about the workings of science made the evenings one of the most exciting entertainments for a Friday night.

For the first Friday Evening Discourse on February 3, 1826, Faraday demonstrated the properties of "caoutchouc," natural rubber. A Scotsman, Charles Macintosh, had patented a waterproof fabric covered with the material. His invention, the raincoat, is today in some places called a mackintosh. Faraday spoke on the chemistry of caoutchouc, its uses, and experiments he had performed on it.

For other Friday Evening Discourses, Faraday discussed topics such as an engine that ran on carbon dioxide, lithography, manufacture of pens, oriental gongs, and sound. Other speakers lectured and demonstrated new discoveries from their fields of work.

In a letter to Captain Franklin, Faraday described the lectures. "[We] . . . have established conversaziones on Friday Evenings which have been numerously and well attended. We light up the house, bring forward a subject in the Lecture room illustrated by experiments, diagrams, models &c, and this serves as Matter for the Evening. We then adjourn to the library where we take tea and seldom part till 11 o'clock or past."

Faraday had years before compiled a list of conditions for a good lecture. Over the course of several letters to his friend, Benjamin Abbott, he discussed the lighting, the time to have a lecture, the design of a lecture room, and the manner of the speaker. "The most prominent requisite to a lecturer, though perhaps not really the most important, is a good delivery; . . . yet I am sorry to say that the generality of mankind cannot accompany us one short hour unless the path is strewed with flowers." He adds that a speaker may write out his lecture, but it should never just be read. Capturing the audience's attention at the beginning is critical, but the interest must be maintained throughout the lecture. "A flame should be lighted

Faraday lecturing at the Royal Institution *(Courtesy of The Royal Institution/ The Bridgeman Art Library)*

at the commencement and kept alive with unremitting splendour to the end."

Other advice for a lecturer: "If at a loss for a word, not to ch-ch-ch or eh-eh-eh, but to stop and wait for it. It soon comes . . . " And "A lecturer should appear easy & collected . . . his whole behavior should evince respect for his audience and he should in no case forget that he is in their presence."

Faraday's niece, Margery Reid, recalled that her uncle had a card with the word "slow" written in large letters placed on the lecture table to remind himself to speak slowly and distinctly. He also had a card with "time" on it to warn him of the end of the hour.

Through the Friday Evening Discourses, Faraday hoped not only to save the Royal Institution, but to transfer some of his excitement about science to the general public, bringing about scientific literacy. He declared, "I am persuaded that all persons may find in natural things an admirable school for self-instruction, and a field for the necessary mental exercise; that they may easily apply their habits of thought, thus formed, to a social use: and that they ought to do this, as a duty to themselves and their generation."

As the Industrial Revolution grew and flourished in England, people became intrigued by technology and science. Huge steam engines running mills and train engines were the high tech of the day and the Friday Evening Discourses tapped into this curiosity.

A London newspaper, the *Literary Gazette,* praised the Discourses, calling them "the most rational and pleasurable assemblies which are to be found in London." Faraday delivered 123 of the Friday Discourses and others spoke as well. John Dalton spoke on his atomic theory; Charles Lyell on volcanoes; Richard Owen on gorillas; and James Clerk Maxwell on the theory of primary colors. Audiences ranged from about four hundred up to the limit of the room at about one thousand.

The popularity of the Friday Evening Discourses guaranteed the success of the fundraising efforts, and before long the Royal Institution was headed back to financial stability. Faraday turned his attention to lectures for another audience, children.

In 1826, Faraday initiated a series of Christmas Juvenile lectures. The first one, presented by his friend Professor J. Wallis, was on astronomy. The next year, Faraday delivered a six-lesson series on chemistry. Through the years, he presented lectures on electricity, metals, and combustion. Always

Faraday would invite guest lecturers like naturalist Richard Owen to the Royal Institution's Friday Evening Discourses.

he included experiments and demonstrations to show his young listeners the wonders of science.

Faraday's wonder and curiosity shined through his lectures, as he was filled with joy and childlike wonder when discussing science. In one he says "I claim the privilege of speaking to juveniles as a juvenile myself."

One of Faraday's most popular lectures, "The Chemical History of a Candle," has become a classic chemistry demonstration. Many chemistry teachers of today begin a lab course with a similar demonstration.

The candle lectures began with Faraday describing different types of candles, displaying common candles, candles from Japan, and even a type of wood from the bogs of Ireland that burns much like a candle. He explained how candles were made and then showed the children candles that came in interesting shapes and colors. Whetting their interest, he stated that he would show why the interesting shapes don't make a superior candle. Then he drew their attention to the flame of a candle and used a glass globe to keep air currents away from the flame, making the top of the candle into a perfectly shaped bowl. He explained that the cup is formed by heated air moving upward all around the candle top and then cooling along the edges.

Faraday showed the action of the wick as it drew up wax by capillary action. Using a column of salt and colored salt solution, he explained how capillary action pulls the solution up the column. The flame doesn't burn down the length of the wick because it is extinguished by the melted wax in the bowl. He then explained the shape and color of the flame.

One remarkable demonstration is of matter rising from the candle. Faraday placed a lit candle in front of a piece of white paper and focused a bright light or the sun on the candle. An image of the candle, wick and flame appeared on the paper. "Curiously enough, however, what we see in the shadow as the darkest part of the flame is, in reality, the brightest part; and here you see streaming upward the ascending current of hot air . . . which draws out the flame, supplies it with air, and cools the sides of the cup of melted fuel."

Faraday demonstrated the importance of fresh air to a candle's flame and proceeded to burn combustible materials such as gunpowder and iron filings. He gave his listeners a warning, "let me hope that none of you, by trying to repeat them [these experiments] for fun's sake, will do any harm." In other words, don't try this at home.

In Lectures 3 and 4, Faraday demonstrated experiments that prove that water is produced by the flame of a candle and then continued to teach about changes of state from water to ice and water to steam. Then he broke the water obtained into its components of oxygen and hydrogen and repeated that these elements came from the flame of the candle. Air was the next substance to be deconstructed into oxygen, nitrogen, and carbon dioxide.

Toward the end of Lecture 6, Faraday compared the flame of a candle with processes in the human body. "Now I must take you to a very interesting part of our subject—to the relation between the combustion of a candle and that living kind of combustion which goes on within us. In every one of us there is a living process of combustion going on very similar to that of a candle."

Throughout his lectures, Faraday encouraged the children to be observant and curious, characteristics of a scientist. He said, "We come here to be philosophers [scientists], and I hope you will always remember that whenever a result happens, especially if it be new, you should say, 'What is the cause? Why does it occur?' and you will, in the course of time, find out the reason."

Charles Dickens, author of *A Christmas Carol* and *David Copperfield,* urged Faraday to publish his Christmas lectures. Faraday didn't want to detract from the lecture version, so

Charles Dickens *(Library of Congress)*

he declined. However, transcripts of two of the lecture series were made: "The Chemical History of A Candle" and "Forces of Matter."

The lecture on forces, one of Faraday's last, was presented in 1859. By this time, he had speculated about the different forces seen in the world and their connection to each other. He began the lecture by reminding his audience of the wonder of how we stand on this world. The force that keeps us upright is usually ignored. He then demonstrated static electricity and pronounces that it is also a force or a power. "We are not to suppose that there are so very many different powers; on the contrary, it is wonderful to think how few are the powers by which all the phenomena of nature are governed."

He asked the audience: "Why do I hold the bottle above the vessel to pour the water into it? You will say, because experience has taught me that it is necessary. I do it for a better reason because it is a law of nature that the water should fall toward the earth . . . that power is what we call gravity."

In the next two lectures, he explained the power of cohesion—particles of bodies sticking together and how that attraction can be weakened by heat. Using an iron bar, he showed how it can be bent after heating because the heat has lessened the attraction of the iron particles. Water turns into ice because the decrease of temperature increases the attraction of the water particles. Steam comes from a decrease of attraction.

From the attraction of particles, he moved into attraction of different types of particles. For example, in water, particles of hydrogen and oxygen are attracted into one molecule. He proceeded with several demonstrations of chemical reactions and then stated, "I want you to observe that one great exertion of this power which is known as chemical affinity is to produce Heat and light." This combination shows that one force can often result in the formation of another.

In his fifth lecture on forces, Faraday explained the dual nature of magnetism and electricity. The duality is seen in the fact that magnetism and electricity both repel and attract. One striking example of this is a bar magnet. Each end of a bar magnet will attract a metallic key, but the center will not. However, if the magnet is cut in two, the part that had been the center and not attracting the key will now cause the key to stick. "Here is a little fragment which I have broken out of the very centre of the bar, and you will see that one end is attractive and the other is repulsive. Now is not this power a most wonderful thing?"

Faraday showed how different the transmission of the force of heat is from the transmission of electricity. While electricity zooms simultaneously through a wire, heat applied to one end of a metal bar requires time to reach the other end of the bar.

At the end of the last lecture, Faraday mentioned the relationship seen between electricity and magnetism—the one he helped establish.

> Philosophers have been suspecting this affinity [relationship] for a long time, and had long had great hopes of success; for in the pursuit of science we first start with hopes and expectations; these we realize and establish, never again to be lost, and upon them we found new expectations of farther discoveries, and so go on pursuing, realizing, establishing, and founding new hopes again and again.

Children that attended Faraday's lectures treasured the memory of them. One person said, "He made us all laugh heartily; and when he threw a coalscuttle full of coals, a poker, and a pair of tongs at the great magnet, and they stuck there, the theatre echoed with shouts of laughter." Alfred Yarrow, later a famous English shipbuilder, remembered, "At the end of the lectures at the Royal Institution, Faraday used to stop sometimes for quite half an hour talking to a lot of us boys, and sometimes making us go through some of his own experiments with our own hands."

While delivering his lectures, Faraday felt obligated to accept a research project from Sir Davy, his former mentor. Starting in 1825 and lasting for six years, he studied the properties and manufacture of optical glass used for telescopes. German scientists were making superb lenses and Englishmen wanted to catch up. The research was long and arduous for Faraday. He tried numerous combinations of ingredients to perfect the glass. However, even if ingredients for a good product were used, often the mixture would heat unevenly or cool too quickly, ruining a batch that had taken hours to prepare. One result of this research was a type of glass known as polarizing glass which would come in handy in later years.

In 1827, Faraday received an offer to become chemistry professor at the University of London. After contemplation, he turned down the offer, saying, "The [Royal] Institution has been a source of knowledge and pleasure to me for the past fourteen years . . . and I remember the protection it has afforded me during the past years of my scientific life."

He did become a part-time professor of chemistry at the Royal Military Academy at Woolwich. Classes of future officers learned chemistry basics from him.

By the summer of 1828, Faraday's heavy schedule of research, analyses for customers, and lectures had worn him out. He began to have severe headaches and weakness, and so decided it was time for a vacation. For two months, he and Sarah roamed the countryside and enjoyed time at a seaside cottage. The rest of his life, these times of complete rest were needed periodically so he could continue his scientific work. His greatest scientific discovery was just ahead.

six

The Discovery of Electromagnetism

*I*n early 1831, Faraday conducted a group of experiments on vibrations. Using a long, flexible board, he placed different substances on pans and caused them to vibrate. No scientific conclusions seem to come from these experiments, at least in the short term. However, Faraday was fascinated by the different patterns he saw. He tested chemicals, minerals, and substances found around his home. From heaps of sand placed on the vibrating surface, star shapes appeared. "This is exceedingly beautiful," he wrote. Egg white and oil accumulated in the center of the pan when vibrated.

Faraday performed some of the experiments in sunlight, apparently to enjoy the sparkling effects. In his laboratory notebook with each paragraph numbered, he wrote:

> 98. Mercury on tin plate being vibrated in sunshine gave very beautiful effects of reflection.

101. Ink and water vibrated in sunshine looked extremely beautiful.

In some experiments, vibrations on one plate could induce vibrations on a nearby plate. A force was being transmitted from one substance to another. This idea of induction, one event causing another to occur, would be the foundation of Faraday's biggest achievement.

Faraday had read a report from Augustin Fresnel about the possibility that light occurred in waves. Much earlier in 1801, Englishman Thomas Young had also proposed that light came in waves, not particles. The attack on this idea was so strong, though, that he withdrew the idea. Fresnel postulated that light emanates from a source like waves from a stone thrown into a pond. The wave traveled through matter without carrying matter along with it. Faraday probably began to speculate that electricity might travel in a similar fashion.

During a seaside holiday with Sarah, Faraday noticed some of the same patterns in the sand along the shore. He noticed that the ridges of sand form parallel to the direction of the wind. Jumping from the appearance of the pattern to a practical application, he suggested that "they may serve to indicate how the wind has been during a night."

After a relatively quiet time in his laboratory and a vacation, Faraday was prepared to make the biggest discovery of his life. Ten years after his discovery of electromagnetic rotation, Faraday was returning to the study of electricity and magnetism.

In the years since his work on electromagnetic rotation, he had performed a few experiments with the reciprocal idea: if electricity could produce magnetism, why couldn't magnetism

Aug 29th 1831.

1. Expts on the production of Electricity from Magnetism &c
2. Have had an iron ring made (soft iron), iron round and inches thick & ring 6 inches in external diameter — Wound many coils of copper wire round one half the coils being separated by twine & calico — there were 3 lengths of wire each about 24 feet long and they could be connected as one length or used as separate lengths. By trial with a trough each was insulated from the other. Will call this side of the Ring A. on the other side but separated by an interval was wound wire in two pieces together amounting to about 60 feet in length the direction being as with the former coils this side call B.

Charged a battery of 10 pr plates 4 inches square. Made the coil on B side one coil and connected its extremities by a copper wire passing to a distance and just over a magnetic needle (3 feet from iron ring) then connected the ends of one of the pieces on A side with battery. Immediately a sensible effect on needle. It oscillated & settled at last in original position. On breaking connection of A side with Battery again a disturbance of the needle.

Made all the wires on A side one coil and sent current from battery through the whole. Effect on needle much stronger than before —

The effect on the needle then but a very small part of that which the wire communicating directly with the battery could produce

produce electricity? He knew that an iron bar wrapped in wire becomes a magnet when current passes through the wire. He carried a tiny wire-wrapped iron cylinder in his pocket and occasionally was seen turning it over between his fingers and studying it.

In early August 1831, he asked his assistant, Charles Anderson, to forge an iron ring six inches in diameter and ⅞ of an inch thick. After the ring was formed, Faraday carefully wrapped one hemisphere of the ring with three lengths of copper wire, each twenty-four inches long. This side he designated side A. To insulate the wire, he added pieces of fabric and twine. Then he wound sixty feet of copper wire around the matching hemisphere, side B, also insulating it as he went.

On Monday, August 29, 1831, Faraday was ready to experiment with his wrapped ring. He started a new section in his

Instruments Faraday used in his experiments with electromagnetism, including an iron ring wrapped with copper wire (4) that he used to convert magnetism to electricity. (*Courtesy of Hulton Archive/Getty Images*)

notebook with paragraph one and headed it "Expts. On the production of Electricity from Magnetism, etc. etc." He connected a battery to wires coming from side A of the ring and the wires of side B ran to a small compass. By this apparatus he could detect if any current flowed in side B when current was present in side A. The magnetic needle would deflect if electricity was present.

When the side A wire was connected to the battery, the compass needle "oscillated and settled at last in original position." When the battery was disconnected, the needle again jumped: Faraday had induced current in side B. What Faraday had constructed with his wire wrapped ring was a transformer. A ring with wires wrapped around each hemisphere can be used to vary the amount of power available on each side. For example, electricity comes into a home at 220 volts, but most items such as radios or CD players can run on nine volts. A transformer inside the electronics reduces the power to nine volts. Outside, large gray cylinders are mounted near electrical lines. These are transformers that reduce the power coming from the electric company to the 220 volts that enter a home.

Faraday had more experiments in his mind, but he and Sarah had planned a vacation at a seaside cottage. As always, they rode on the top of the coach when they left on their trip. Huddled in their raincoats, they enjoyed the fresh air and sights of the countryside instead of being cooped up inside with other passengers.

Soon after arriving at the cottage, he wrote to Richard Phillips, referring to but not yet explaining his electromagnetic experiments. "I am busy just now again on electromagnetism, and think I have got hold of a good thing, but can't say. It may be a weed instead of a fish that, after all my labour, I may at last pull up."

While relaxing at the seaside, Faraday wound several more coils to have ready for future experiments. He used different types of metal wire and wound the coils in a variety of ways, designating them as coils A to L.

After returning to London, Faraday took a few days to clear his desk of piled up work. Then on Saturday, September 24, he was ready to go back to electromagnetism experiments. One by one, he connected his A to L coils to the battery and measured the jumps of the needle. Some combinations produced no twitches, others jumped and returned. In the late day, he tied two bar magnets into a V-shaped jaw, like a pair of tweezers. He placed a wire wrapped iron bar between the jaws and attached the ends of the wire to a galvanometer, an instrument for measuring current. When he opened the jaws of the magnets, the galvanometer needle jumped. When he closed the jaws, the needle jumped the opposite direction. For his last notebook entry, he wrote, "Hence here distinct conversion of Magnetism into Electricity."

To prove that the electricity induced in the secondary coil was ordinary electricity like that from a battery, Faraday conducted a series of experiments. He attached metal or carbon electrodes to the coil and touched them to his tongue, expecting to feel the familiar shock of electricity. There was none. He tried to decompose an acidic solution with the electrodes. Nothing happened. The induced electricity was too short-lived to observe any of these electrical tests. He was able to magnetize a needle and produce a spark from the side B coil.

In October 1831, Faraday changed the shape of the coil. Using a stiff paper to form a cylinder, he wrapped wire around the paper making a tunnel of wire and paper. Into the cavity of the tunnel, he thrust a bar magnet and then pulled it out. When the magnet was either moving into the tunnel or coming out, the galvanometer needle jumped, indicating electrical induction in the wires. When the magnet was moved back and forth outside the cylinder, nothing happened. The combination of tunnel of wire and bar magnet was the discovery that scientists had been searching for. But the brief induction was not enough. Faraday had more work to do to bring electricity to the public.

He traveled to the site of the huge horseshoe magnet owned by the Royal Society. This gigantic and powerful magnet consisted of 437 bar magnets bound together so they functioned as one magnet. A one-hundred-pound force was necessary to yank an iron bar from the magnet.

When Faraday placed an iron rod into the tunnel of his wire wrapped cylinder and touched the rod to the huge magnet, the galvanometer needle fluctuated wildly. It even deflected when the rod was approaching the magnet. Faraday had proved his hypothesis that inducing current required a change of magnetism, not just the presence of magnetism.

Faraday's next experiment had been inspired by a device known as Arago's wheel. French scientist Francois Arago had demonstrated that a disk of nonmagnetic metal becomes magnetic when it spins. No one could explain how magnetism could arise in a disk of metals such as copper. But Faraday determined to solve the mystery.

He had brought a twelve-inch copper disk attached to an axle. Galvanometer leads were placed on the disk and the disk was spun between the arms of the huge magnet. The galvanometer needle swung to the side and stayed there. When the

A sketch in Faraday's diary of the copper disk and magnet apparatus he used to produce a steady electrical current. *(Library of Congress)*

disk was spun in the opposite direction, the needle also swung to the other side and stayed. Faraday had produced a steady current using a spinning disk in a magnetic field. Magnetism had induced a flow of current. Faraday invented the first electric dynamo or electric generator, which today is the principal to produce electric current. At age forty, Faraday added to the power of the Industrial Revolution by providing electricity, ushering in the Electric Age.

How did the dynamo work? The magnet was not being turned on and shut off or moved like the tweezers experiment. The magnetic field surrounding the magnet stayed the same. However, the field around a magnet is not uniform. The pull of magnetism is greatest around the poles, less toward the center. As the disk spun, it rotated through different strengths of the magnetic field, inducing electricity.

Faraday's invention caused a stir among scientists and even politicians. The prime minister of England, Robert Peel, saw a demonstration of the dynamo and asked what the use of it might be. Faraday replied, "I know not, but I wager that one day your government will tax it."

For Faraday, the thrill of discovery was enough. He didn't desire to develop the practical applications of his invention.

Grand Coulee Dam

One of the largest power plants in the United States is at Grand Coulee Dam on the Columbia River in Washington state. Four powerhouses generate 6470 megawatts of electricity, making it the largest producer of hydroelectric power. The method used by the power generators is Faraday's electromagnetic induction.

The Grand Coulee Dam *(Courtesy of U.S. Bureau of Reclamation)*

He said, "I have rather . . . been desirous of discovering new facts and new relations dependent on magneto-electric induction, than of exalting the force of those already obtained; being assured that the latter would find their full development hereafter."

Faraday's lack of understanding of higher mathematics had not prevented his greatest discovery. In a letter to his friend, Richard Phillips, Faraday's usual humble attitude breaks into a moment of pride when he writes, "It is quite comfortable to me to find that experiment need not quail before mathematics, but is quite competent to rival it in discovery." He continued that he was writing up his inventions and ideas in a paper entitled *Experimental Researches in Electricity.*

Unfortunately for Faraday, his latest discovery did not escape controversy. Soon after his experiments with the huge magnet and copper disk, he wrote to his French friend, J. N. P. Hachette about his results. Hachette gave the letter to Francois Arago who had it read at a meeting of the Academy of Sciences in Paris. A French magazine published an incorrect account and added that the principle of induction had been discovered by Frenchmen. Two Italian scientists read the magazine article and published their own paper, giving Faraday the credit for the discovery. Even though their article was written in 1832, well after Faraday's discovery, it had the date of November 1831 on it, implying that they had discovered the dynamo before Faraday. The publisher of the *Literary Gazette* in London printed news that the Italians had made the discovery and Faraday had "repeated" the experiments. Faraday immediately fired off a letter to the editor of the *Literary Gazette* stating "I never took more pains to be quite independent of others persons than in the present investigation; and I have never been more annoyed about any paper than the present by the variety of circumstances which have arisen seeming to imply that I had been anticipated." The paper printed an apology, and Hachette also wrote apologizing for setting the entire controversy into motion; "To render you complete justice, to assure you all priority, was my only aim."

The confusion over the date of discovery continued to haunt Faraday as he had announced his invention to the Royal Society on November 24, 1831, but the paper of the discovery was not printed until 1832. He learned his lesson: never release results before publication of the scientific paper.

In spite of the controversy, Faraday's claim to priority stands and today he is acknowledged as the person who made electromagnetic induction work. The Royal Society awarded him its highest award, the Copley Medal.

Also, in 1832 at the second meeting of the British Association for the Advancement of Science, Faraday was granted an honorary degree of Doctor of Civil Law from Oxford University.

Faraday was not finished with electrical and magnetic inventions. His paper on induction described magnetic lines of force. He spoke of the induction coming from "cutting" or crossing these lines. He began to think about inducing electricity with the earth, the biggest magnet accessible to man.

By rotating a large wire loop, he showed an electrical current formed from the earth's magnetic field. He wondered if the rotation of the earth would be enough to induce current in a wire. He would need a large body of water to provide a material different in conductivity from metals to produce the electricity. After obtaining permission, Faraday strung a long wire through the large pond at Kensington Gardens. A slight current was detected, but Faraday realized that probably was due to impurities in the water, not induction. He repeated his experiment in the moving water of the Thames River, but it also failed. He envisioned stringing wire across the English Channel, but was unable to conduct the experiment. Years later, the current he expected was found in underwater telegraph cables.

As Faraday's eminence as a scientist grew, some of his friends attempted to convince the English government to provide a pension for him. They persuaded the prime minister that England should honor Faraday, but before the matter could be settled, the government changed. The Tories were voted out and a Whig government was in place. When Faraday heard of the scheme, he was not pleased anyway. He felt that he had no need of money from the government when he could still work. Besides, his Sandemanian beliefs compelled him to stay out of politics. Eventually, in later years, he did accept a small pension from the government.

In the meantime, Faraday continued his work.

seven

Faraday's Laws

After the discovery of electrical induction, Faraday decided that the study of electricity needed new terms. With the help of William Whewell, a science historian, he coined words still used today: electrode, anode, cathode, ion, electrolyte, and electrolysis. Other scientists were not pleased with the new nomenclature at first, but gradually it came into popular use.

About the same time, the word scientist came into use; previously, those who worked in the sciences were called natural philosophers. Faraday liked the word, but disliked the new term physicist. He wrote to Whewell, "'physicist' is both to my mouth & ears so awkward that I think I shall never be able to use it. The equivalent of three separate sounds in *s* in one word is too much."

Faraday performing an experiment with electrolysis. *(Courtesy of Mary Evans Picture Library/Alamy)*

Faraday was intrigued by the difference in the conduction of electricity through solids and liquids. For instance, water will conduct electricity, but frozen water—ice—will not. In other words, water is a conductor while ice is an insulator (does not conduct). Faraday wondered why the same chemical would produce different results by the change of state.

After investigating other substances, Faraday found several others that behave as water does. For example, sodium chloride conducts electricity when it is dissolved in water or melted. But solid sodium chloride does not conduct electricity. He found another common property of these substances. When electricity passes through one of these substances in solution, the substance decomposes at the electrodes. If, as some scientists still contended, electricity was an imponderable fluid, not reacting with surrounding matter, it should not be affected by whether the matter was solid or liquid.

Today scientists understand that sodium chloride breaks into ions in solution. When electricity is applied, sodium metal accumulates at the negative electrode while chlorine bubbles up at the positive. In solid sodium chloride, the ions are chained in place; Faraday came to understand through his work and experimentation, though was unable to articulate it so clearly.

Other scientists perceived the electrical forces tearing apart the molecules found in solution. Faraday saw that movement of charged particles completes the electrical current and the electrically charged particles are attracted to the opposite electrode. To prove that the presence of electrodes was not necessary, he zapped a piece of acid-soaked paper with static electricity propagated through air. The solution showed decomposition, demonstrating that electrodes were not needed for the process of breakdown to occur.

His experiments demonstrated that decomposition and current worked hand in hand.

> Those bodies which, being interposed between the metals of the voltaic pile, render it active, *are all of them electrolytes;* and it cannot but press upon the attention of every one engaged in considering this subject, that in those bodies (so essential to the pile) decomposition and the transmission of a current are so intimately connected, that one cannot happen without the other. This I have shown abundantly in water, and numerous other cases.

Faraday contemplated the process of electrolysis. Sir Humphry Davy and others had advanced the field of electro-chemistry using batteries. Davy had isolated metals such as sodium, potassium, and calcium by passing electrical current through melted salts of these compounds. With a steady source of electricity possible from his dynamo, Faraday studied the electrolysis process extensively. His conclusions came to be known as Faraday's Laws of Electrolysis:

> 1. Chemical action or decomposition is exactly proportional to the amount of electricity applied.
> 2. Electrochemical equivalents are the same as ordinary chemical equivalents.

As stated in *Experimental Researches in Electricity,*

> That for a constant quantity of electricity, whatever the decomposing conductor may be, whether water, saline solutions, acids, fused bodies, etc., the amount of electro-chemical action is also a constant quality, i.e. would always be equivalent to a standard chemical effect founded upon ordinary chemical affinity.

A unit was named for Faraday's electrolysis work. The faraday measures the amount of electricity transferred per equivalent weight of the element deposited.

Faraday's contemporary, English scientist John Dalton, had shown that matter consists of atoms that combine in specific proportions to form molecules. Faraday showed that both matter and electricity occur in discrete units. He also proved that the electricity from static charges, batteries or induction are the same and so by rule #2, decompose the same amount of matter. Today, it is known that Faraday's Laws work because

John Dalton (*Library of Congress*)

electricity is the movement of electrons that surround atoms. So Faraday's Laws linking electricity and chemical properties is actually a way of measuring the number of electrons involved in the reaction.

Electrolysis is used in many industries today, including silver-plating spoons and jewelry, applying chrome to steel for cars, and sticking tin to iron for cans to hold food.

Faraday also stated a law for the relationship between the concentration of magnetic lines of force and the amount of electricity induced in a coil.

Faraday returned to experiments with static electricity to disprove the theory of electrical fluids. If electrical fluids exist, then the inside of a charged vessel would show a charge. Also, an item could be charged without the charge being lost in surroundings. Faraday planned to prove that the opposite was true. He hypothesized that charged vessels would remain electrically neutral inside and that when an item received a charge, an opposite but equal amount of charge would appear somewhere else.

Using an electrostatic machine, Faraday charged the outside of vessels made of various metals. With a sensitive probe stuck through holes of the vessels, he found that the charge stayed on the exterior of the vessels, not inside. Nearby objects became charged with the opposite charge. There was only an equal amount of overall charge.

Then he constructed what came to be known as Faraday's Cage. A wooden box, twelve feet on a side was built and covered with copper wire and tin, creating a conductive surface. The box was supported by insulating blocks. When the outside was charged by an electrostatic generator, the inside stayed charge free. To prove this, Faraday entered the box. He wrote, "I went into the cube and lived in it, and using lighted candles, electrometers, and all other tests of electrical states, I could not find the least influence upon them, or indication of anything particular given by them, though all the time the outside of the cage was powerfully charged, and large sparks and brushes were darting off from every part of its outer surface."

Both cars and airplanes function as Faraday's Cages. If struck by lightning or another electrical charge, occupants inside the vehicles are safe because the charge is dissipated by the metallic outside.

Faraday's Cage demolished the idea of electricity as a fluid. From this time on, it was regarded as a force. But other fallacies were still believed by many scientists. One was the "action at a distance" idea. The theory stated that force is transmitted instantaneously from a source to an object. Already with his description of magnetic lines of force, Faraday had attacked the idea. If his theory was right, lines of force emanated from electrical, magnetic, and gravitational bodies would demolish the action at a distance idea completely. Proving that the transmission of the forces occurred over time, even as short as a millisecond, would finish off the idea of instantaneous action at a distance.

He had concentric spheres built of metal nested together with a space in between. Into the gap he placed materials such as wax, glass, sulfur, and shellac. When the spheres were charged, the materials in the gap were also charged. Faraday named these substances dielectrics because they would display negative charges on one side and positive on the other. For example, a piece of glass placed between the two spheres would not have a change of the total charge, but negative charges would line up on one side and positive on the other.

This dielectric quality allowed the spheres to store electricity. When a charge was applied to the outer sphere, the charge passed through the dielectric and to the inner sphere. Once the outer sphere was discharged, it became recharged by drawing electricity from the inner sphere through the dielectric material. The action at a distance theory saw only forces at the conducting spheres, ignoring the dielectric medium. When Faraday showed that the medium also had a role in the conduction of electricity, the action at a distance theory was dead.

Faraday reckoned that the transmittance of electricity occurred particle to particle. Therefore, it required some time. As his biographer and friend, John Tyndall wrote, "Faraday figured their particles as polarized, and he concluded that the force of induction is propagated from particle to particle of the dielectric from the inner sphere to the outer one. This power of propagation possessed by insulators he called their '*Specific Inductive Capacity.*'"

Faraday's design of concentric spheres with a dielectric in the gap is now known as a capacitor, and it is present in every electronic device one can name. A unit called the farad measures the amount of storage available in a capacitor.

The experiments with the spheres convinced Faraday that the distinction between conductors and insulators was a matter of degrees. He believed that the ease of conductance depended on the amount of "strain" that the molecules of a substance could bear. Metals can bear only a tiny strain before electricity flows, so they are good conductors. Other materials, called insulators, withstand a lot of strain before current passes through them. However, under enough strain, even good insulators will allow electricity to flow.

Various types of capacitors

Faraday conducted one other set of experiments that finished off the action at a distance theory. The theory stated that force always travels in a straight line or as Tyndall wrote: "Gravity . . . will not turn a corner." Experiments showed that a sphere could be charged electrically by the approach of a charged sphere even with an obstacle between them. Electrical force could turn a corner. Maybe magnetic and gravitational forces could do the same.

In November and December 1837, Faraday read his eleventh section of *Experimental Researches in Electricity* to the Royal Society. At the beginning, he stated his certainty about the importance of electricity, experimentation, and an open mind.

> The science of electricity is in that state in which every part of it requires experimental investigation; not merely for the discovery of new effects, but what is just now of far more importance, the development of the means by which the old effects are produced, and the consequent more accurate determination of the first principles of action of the most extraordinary and universal power in nature: and to those philosophers [scientists] who pursue the inquiry zealously yet cautiously, combining experiment with analogy, suspicious of their preconceived notions, paying more respect to a fact than a theory, not too hasty to generalize, and above all things, willing at every step to cross-examine their own opinions, both by reasoning and experiment, no branch of knowledge can afford so fine and ready a field for discovery as this.

In the years since this statement, men such as Thomas Edison, Nikola Tesla, and George Westinghouse have expanded the field of electricity to a ubiquitous presence in our world and our electronics.

In spite of his many accomplishments, some university trained scientists still looked down on Faraday and his lack of formal education. Faraday was aware of his deficiencies, once writing to his friend Ampère, "I am unfortunate in a want of mathematical knowledge and the power of entering with facility into abstract reasoning." However, Faraday still believed in the power of observation and experimentation. As he wrote to John Tyndall, "I have far more confidence in the one man who works mentally and bodily at a matter than in the six who merely talk about it."

A new phenomenon caught Faraday's attention—photography. At the Friday Evening Discourse at the Royal Institution on January 25, 1839, Faraday spoke about the new process. He

Scientists like Thomas Edison (above) and George Westinghouse used Faraday's ground-breaking experiments with electricity as a platform for their own discoveries. *(Library of Congress)*

showed examples sent to him by Henry Fox Talbot and both credited Frenchman Louis-Jacques Daguerre with simultaneous discovery of the process.

Faraday was interested in the chemical techniques of photography and tested them in his laboratory. He also had many photographs taken. From 1840 to the 1860s, he was one of the most photographed figures.

In the late 1830s, Faraday's health worsened. His headaches and weakness increased. He confided to friend Christian Friedrich Schoenbein that his "memory [was] so treacherous that I cannot remember the beginning of a sentence to the end."

In November of 1839, he suffered from attacks of vertigo. As was standard medicine at the time, his doctor bled him and ordered him to rest and relax his mind. Faraday began to turn down all social invitations, and he and Sarah traveled to Brighton for an extended vacation. In a letter to a nephew, Sarah wrote, "your Uncle is pretty well but not so strong as I should like to see him, he often needs relaxation."

His laboratory notebook recorded only five days of work from January 11 to February 11, 1840. Then there is another gap of time until five more days in August and then no more entries until June of 1842.

In the summer of 1841, the Faradays and Sarah's brother, George Barnard and wife Emma, spent three months in Switzerland and Germany. An artist, Barnard would hike into the mountains with pencil and sketching pad. Faraday would usually accompany him. Sarah wrote that he "enjoys the country exceedingly and though at first he lamented on absence from home and friends very much, he seems now to be reconciled to it as a means of improving his general health, his strength is however very good he thinks nothing of walking 30 miles in a day." In his diary, Faraday accounts a hike through a heavy rain, traveling through Gemmi Pass, past the Jungfrau and around a lake to return to the hotel. He had covered forty-five miles in ten and a half hours over rough terrain and returned "in far better condition than I expected . . . After tea I felt a little stiff."

Throughout his life, Faraday's religious life walked hand in hand with his scientific one. The members of the Sandemanian church were as important to him as his scientist friends. He was made a deacon, with the mission of ministering to the physical needs of the members, in 1832.

In 1840, Faraday's spiritual life took a step forward; he was appointed an elder in the church. The office meant that he was considered a spiritual leader, responsible for the souls and welfare of the members of his congregation. In a letter to a fellow elder of the Edinburgh church, he wrote about a member suffering from health problems: "she is very patient & comforted by the scriptures in the great & glorious hope of relief not merely from these things but from all sorrow & sighing through Jesus Christ and rejoices in her friends company."

As an elder, Faraday was expected to preach sermons at some services. From surviving cards, it is clear his sermon techniques were influenced by his lecture experience. He filled his sermon with examples from both Old and New Testaments and expounded on characteristics that God desired his followers to have.

On March 31, 1844, Faraday was excluded from the Sandemanian church. The usual reason give by his biographers is that he was invited to dine with Queen Victoria on a

Sunday. The situation caused a conflict for the Sandemanian who was expected to attend every service of the church, but also required to be a loyal citizen. When questioned by the congregation, Faraday was not repentant, but defended his actions in visiting the Queen and missing services. Faraday's earliest biographer, John H. Gladstone, writes that his unrepentant heart, not the action, caused his exclusion. By excluding him, the church took the eldership away from him and also refused to associate with him for a time.

However, records of the London congregation show that Faraday was not the only one excluded on that March Sunday. Eighteen others, including his brother Robert, sister-in-law, Margaret and father-in-law, Edward Barnard, were also put out of the congregation. It seems probable that the conflict was more than a visit to the Queen on a Sunday. The congregation and the whole Sandemanian church were facing several divisive issues at the time, so more likely the exclusion came from a stand taken by the eighteen members against the rest of the congregation. Also, there is no evidence from Faraday that he visited the Queen. The exclusion lasted until May 5, about five weeks, but Faraday felt it deeply. He wrote to Schoebein that he was particularly "low in health and spirits." Once Faraday and most of the others had expressed repentance, they were allowed back into full fellowship with the congregation. But Faraday was not an elder again for sixteen more years.

Faraday believed strongly in God, but also had great faith in science. He reconciled the two by his fervent view of God as creator of everything. In an 1844 memorandum on the nature of matter, he declared that "God has been pleased to work in his material creation by laws." He stressed that the job of a scientist was to discover the laws by which God ruled

An 1850 photograph of Faraday *(Courtesy of The Print Collector/Alamy)*

the world. "How wonderful it is to me the simplicity of nature when we rightly interpret her laws." He wrote "But though the natural works of God . . . ever glorify him still I do not think it at all necessary to tie the study of the natural science & religion together and in my intercourse with my fellow creatures that which is religious & that which is philosophical have ever been two distinct things."

The early 1840s were a time of struggle for Faraday. Conflicts with his church, and concerns over his health and mental state and lack of direction in his scientific pursuits haunted him. However, some new associations in the next few years would lead him back to science.

eight
Lines of Force

In 1844, Faraday attracted the attention of a famous mathematician. Ada Lovelace, daughter of Lord Byron, became interested in what was called the Analytical Engine invented by Charles Babbage. The Engine was an early ancestor of computers, and Ada wrote what many call the first computer program to make the Engine work.

Ada was a brilliant woman, with a passionate writing style. In her first letter to Faraday, she gushed, "I have long been *vowed to the Temple; –*the Temple of *Truth, Nature, Science!* And every year I take vows more strict . . . bind my very life & soul to *unwearied & undivided* science at it's altars henceforward. I hope to die the *High-Priestess* of God's works as manifested on this earth."

Faraday reminded her in a return letter that she was in her youth while he was "a labourer of many years' standing made

Ada Lovelace

daily to feel my wearing out." The correspondence between the two continued for a while. In one, Ada asks if there is something she can do for Faraday when she visited another scientist saying, "I would not miss a possible opportunity of being useful to *you,* or useful to Science, (*Science whose bride* I am)!"

Ada corresponded with many men of science and she was able to converse with them fluently in scientific terms. Her ardent passion may have startled and yet flattered Faraday. Eventually her ardor became too much and Faraday calmed the relationship until there was no contact between them. She died of cancer in 1852 at the age of thirty-seven.

Experiments on electricity, magnetism, gravity, and light led Faraday to visualize connections between all forces. Eventually his view came down to the atomic level. John Dalton, another English scientist, had proposed that atoms were tiny, round balls surrounded by empty space. Faraday's work with electricity led him to disagree with Dalton's theory.

Faraday agreed that atoms must be surrounded by space and not touching one another because otherwise, they would not be compressible. Gases can be squeezed into much smaller volumes because of the emptiness between atoms. His disagreement came from the properties of insulation and conduction.

If an atom has a solid mass surrounded by space, then the space is the only continuous part. Metal conducts electricity easily, so the space between the atoms must be where the electricity flows, meaning that the space is a conductor. But in substances such as shellac, an insulator, the space between the atoms must be insulating. How can space be both? In

Faraday's words, "for if space be an insulator it cannot exist in conducting bodies, and if it be a conductor it cannot exist in insulating bodies."

Faraday's solution was to ignore the mass of an atom and concentrate on force. In a Friday Evening Discourse on January 19, 1844, entitled, "A speculation touching Electric Conduction and the Nature of Matter," he said, "All our perception and knowledge of the atom, and even our fancy is limited to ideas of its powers."

Faraday carefully used the word "speculation" in the title, because no one could see an atom at that time. They could only visualize it. For Faraday, the vision was of a web of lines connecting each atom to every other atom in the universe. His atoms are centers of power, not balls of mass. Instead of matter being distinct from space, it was continuous with it. "The powers around the centres give these centres the properties of atoms of matter." Just as there was no distinct line separating insulating materials from conducting materials, there was no line demarking an atom's mass and space.

Dalton's Atomic Theory allowed scientists to visualize individual atoms and their reactions to form molecules. Faraday's lines of force and power ideas put uncertainty into the picture. But both ideas had validity in the long run. In today's concept of subatomic particles, the atom is not a solid mass, but an insubstantial cloud that embodies mass, gravity, and electrical charge.

Faraday believed forces such as magnetism, electricity, and gravity came from the lines of force stretched out from atoms. He realized that these ideas were hard to grasp and even harder to prove by experimentation.

Before the ideas were digested, another young scientist became a friend and correspondent to Faraday. William Thomson, later Lord Kelvin, read Faraday's *Experimental Researches in Electricity* while a student at Cambridge. At first, he was appalled by the lack of mathematical foundation

A suggestion from mathematical physicist Lord Kelvin inspired Faraday to experiment with the relationship between electricity, magnetism, and light.

for Faraday's theories. But then he began to appreciate the work and as he said, became "inoculated with Faraday fire." After meeting Faraday at the annual meeting of the British Association for the Advancement of Science in June 1845, Thomson spent his summer concocting a mathematical model of Faraday's lines of force. Through the equations, he saw experiments that might catapult the theory into reality. On August 5, 1845, he told Faraday that electricity or magnetism should have an impact on light.

Faraday replied that he had tried to observe such an effect, but had only negative results. However, this suggestion from a mathematical scientist inspired Faraday to return to his laboratory and experiments.

Faraday chose to use polarized light for his experiments. Normal light has waves or vibrations that are propagated in all planes. However, when light has vibrations all in one plane it is said to be polarized.

By using polarized light, Faraday had an easy way to determine if light was impacted by electricity or magnets. He obtained polarized light by reflecting the light of a lamp off a piece of glass and then shone the reflected light through a variety of transparent materials and to a polarized lens. The lens was rotated so that none of the polarized light showed. If any was seen, the light was being affected by either electricity or magnetism. Faraday hoped that the transparent material would amplify the effect enough for a difference in the light to be seen.

To start with, Faraday tried a multitude of solutions with electricity running through them. He employed weak current, strong, and current running parallel, perpendicular and in the opposite direction to the light beam. Transparent materials such as air, plate glass, and quartz were placed in the test chamber. His notebook recounts, "no effect"; "still no effect"; "results all negative."

Since he couldn't show electricity impacting light, he switched to magnetism. Using a strong electromagnet, he placed it near the light path and again shone the polarized beam through a plethora of transparent substances. No effect was seen. He tried different strengths of magnets, changed the pole positions, but only found more negative results.

Then finally on September 13, 1845, his notebook contains "BUT" in capital letters and underlined three times. Finally, an interesting result occurred. He could see the image of lamp through the polarizing lens. By turning the electromagnet off and then on, he could make the lamp appear and disappear. The transparent material in the successful experiment was the heavy borate glass that he had used in the optical glass project in the 1820s. The glass had a high refractive value and Faraday realized that this quality magnified the effects of magnetism on light so that he could see the effect. In his notebook he wrote, "This fact will most likely prove exceedingly fertile and of great value in the investigations of . . . conditions of natural force." The effect strengthened the connections between the great forces of electricity, magnetism, and possibly gravity.

Faraday switched to a more powerful electromagnet and tested a variety of substances. His notebook is laced with entries such as "effect was good"; "very fine effect"; and on September 18, 1845, "an excellent day's work."

After showing that magnetism had an effect on light, Faraday wondered about the reverse: could light produce electricity or magnetism? Taking his equipment outside on a sunny day, he tried to detect electricity produced by the light of the sun. The experiment was a failure, but years later photo-electric cells would be built that produce electricity from the light of the sun.

In November 1845, William Thomson published a paper with the first mathematical proof of electrical and magnetic lines of force. He wrote, "All the views which Faraday has brought forward and illustrated or demonstrated by experiment, lead to this method of establishing the mathematical theory." Faraday's lack of mathematical skills had not kept him from proposing a theory that mathematicians could prove by their math.

On April 3, 1846, Charles Wheatstone was supposed to lecture at the Friday Evening Discourse. A shy man, he had apparently panicked at the last minute, leaving Faraday to take his place. Faraday spent a few minutes talking about what he knew about Wheatstone's topic, an electromagnetic stop-watch. Then to fill the rest of the hour, Faraday expounded on a topic that was heavy on his mind, the connection between light and lines of force. The impromptu lecture gave listeners "one of the most singular speculations that ever emanated from a scientific mind."

Thomas Young had shown that light had wave properties, contrary to the idea of light as a particle. One flaw to the theory was that waves require a medium to propagate their energy. What about the emptiness of space? How could light travel through the vacuum from a distant star to earth?

Faraday told his listeners, "The view which I am so bold as to put forth considers . . . radiation as a high species of vibration in the lines of force which are known to connect particles and also masses of matter together."

Later Faraday wrote a letter entitled, "Thought on Ray-vibrations," published in *Philosophical Magazine.* "From first to last, understand that I merely threw out as matter for speculation, the vague impressions of my mind, for I gave nothing as the result of sufficient consideration, or as the settled conviction, or even probable conclusion at which I had arrived."

The lecture and letter provided a glimpse into Faraday's thinking. From his thoughts on ray-vibrations, it becomes apparent that his electrical, magnetic, and gravitational lines of force fill the universe. Each line can be "plucked" to vibrate like a guitar string, propagating force along the line. One conclusion from this model, "The propagation of light and therefore probably of all radiant action, occupies *time;* and, that a vibration of the line of force should account for the phenomena of radiation, it is necessary that such a vibration should occupy time also."

During this time, Faraday also contemplated magnetic lines of force. He coined the term "magnetic field" to describe his vision of the lines emanating from a magnet.

Faraday's ray-vibrations paper provoked criticism, especially from mathematical scientists. However, a new mathematician was coming on the scene.

Scotsman James Clerk Maxwell was born in 1831, the same year that Faraday created electromagnetic induction. As a small boy, Maxwell was always curious. He would ask, "What's the go o' that?" If the answer was not satisfactory, he would ask again, "But what is the *particular* go of it?" After studies at Edinburgh Academy, Maxwell went to Cambridge for college-level classes. After finishing, he became a Fellow at Cambridge in 1854 and began investigating a multitude of natural wonders. The same year, he wrote to William Thomson asking for a list of readings in electricity and magnetism. Soon he was reading Faraday's *Experimental Researches in Electricity.*

Maxwell possessed an extraordinary mathematical mind, and he admired Faraday's work. He wrote, "The method which Faraday employed in his researches consisted in a constant appeal to experiment as a means of testing the truth of

James Clerk Maxwell *(Courtesy of The Print Collector/Alamy)*

his ideas, and a constant cultivation of ideas under the direct influence of experiment . . . " He goes on to recommend "Every student therefore should . . . study Faraday for the cultivation of a scientific spirit, by means of the action and reaction which will take place between newly discovered facts as introduced to him by Faraday and the nascent ideas in his own mind."

Maxwell, meanwhile, cultivated some big ideas of his own. In 1857, he sent one of his papers to Faraday. The title was "On Faraday's Lines of Force." Maxwell had envisioned Faraday's lines of force as fluid-filled tubes and using mathematical equations, prove the validity of Faraday's ideas. The heavy amount of math both intimidated and thrilled Faraday. In a letter back to Maxwell, he wrote, "I was at first almost frightened, when I saw such mathematical force made to bear upon the subject and then wondered to see that the subject stood it so well."

Inspired by Maxwell's work, Faraday went back to work; this time he wanted to study to see if electricity and magnetism take time to move through space. Faraday realized he would face obstacles in this quest. In his notebook, he cataloged the difficulties: "First—the quickness of the action. Second—the great distance therefore required to make the propagation such as to require sensible time—and with that great distance the rapid diminution of the magnetic action that is to be made sensible. Third—the want of instantaneous indicators of magnetic action . . . Fourth—the want of a sudden source of magnetic power." He pressed forward with his experiments, but the obstacles were too large. Thirty years later, Heinrich Hertz finally detected the time delays that Faraday sought.

The experiments led Faraday back to the contemplation of another universal force, gravity. He wrote Maxwell, asking what he thought about gravitational lines of force. Maxwell replied that he believed that Faraday's ideas were valid and that gravitational lines of force could "weave a web across the sky and lead the stars in their courses."

In 1860, Maxwell became a professor at King's College in London. Now that he and Faraday were in the same town, they often met. At one Friday Evening Discourse, Faraday observed Maxwell wending his way through the throng of scientists. He called out, "Ho, Maxwell, cannot you get out? If any man can find a way through a crowd it should be you."

Meantime, Maxwell conjured up another model for electromagnetism. He pictured a set of rollers and cogs with the unusual quality of being able to deform slightly and be pulled out of place. The displacement of one roller or cog pulled the ones closest to it out of place and the effect was propagated in the same way as an electromagnetic wave.

During the summer of 1861, Maxwell derived mathematical formulas to calculate the speed of propagation of an electromagnetic wave. When he finished his equations after his return to London, he found that an electromagnetic wave would travel through air at the speed of 193,088 miles per second—roughly the speed of light.

His work reinforced Faraday's ray-vibrations theory that connected electromagnetism and light. Maxwell wrote, "The electromagnetic theory of light, as proposed by [Faraday], is the same in substance as that which I have begun to develop in this paper, except that in 1846 there were no data to calculate the velocity of propagation."

Maxwell's work on electromagnetism, based on Faraday's theories, led to what is now called field theory. Using his foundation, generations of physicists have expanded the understanding of the relationship between electricity, magnetism, light, heat, and gravity. Albert Einstein would derive the equations for a field theory of gravity nearly one hundred years later. Field theory describing actions at the atomic and subatomic level is now called quantum field theory. Many of the discoveries and advances in physics and electronics today are founded on Maxwell's field theory, which was based on Faraday's work.

In his most famous paper, "A Treatise on Electricity and Magnetism," Maxwell pays tribute to Faraday. "If by anything I have written I may assist any student in understanding Faraday's modes of thought and expression I shall regard it as the accomplishment of one of my principal aims—to communicate to others the same delight which I have found myself in reading Faraday's *Researches*."

While advancing the knowledge of science, Faraday also had to refute some pseudoscience. Table turning parties were being held across London in attempts to communicate with the dead. Participants would stand around a table, resting their hands on its surface. When the table turned, it was considered an answer from the spirits of the dead.

As a foremost scientist, Faraday was asked to investigate the phenomenon. He attended two séances and took along a bundle of things that he thought might transmit or prevent the transmission of the table turning force. He found that the table turning occurred regardless of materials near it. Then he made a lever fastened to a sheet of cardboard that would indicate the direction of pressure placed on the table by the

A table turning party *(Courtesy of Mary Evans Picture Library/Alamy)*

séance participants. He showed that when participants looked at the lever, nothing happened. When they looked away and had no knowledge if the lever was showing pressure to the right or left, the table moved. To Faraday, it was obvious that the phenomenon of table turning was due to the pressure of the hands on the table. In a letter to the *Times,* he attributed the table turning craze to the lack of scientific training. "I think the system of education that could leave the mental condition of the public body in the state in which this subject has found it must have been greatly deficient in some very important principle."

The Royal Institution took up the banner of improving educational methods. Over April and May 1854, a series of lectures was presented by Royal Institution members. Faraday's lecture, entitled "On Mental Education" was attended by Queen Victoria's consort, Prince Albert. He emphasized the importance of training the mind, whether through education or self learning.

Faraday's self learning had brought the world useful electricity, laws of electrolysis, and the foundation of field theory. But his world still had scientific problems that he could illuminate.

nine
Elicit the Truth

In July 1855, Michael Faraday was appalled at the condition of the Thames River that runs through London. In a letter to the *Times,* he described dropping pieces of a white card into its waters and seeing them disappear in the murk "before they had sunk an inch below the surface." He knew that if the river was not cleaned up, the consequences could be severe. "If we neglect this subject, we cannot expect to do so with impunity; nor ought we to be surprised if ere many years are over, a hot season gives us sad proof of the folly of our carelessness."

Faraday knew that a fellow scientist, John Martin, had designed and campaigned for sewage disposal systems that were never built. Cholera outbreaks in 1848-49 and 1854-55 along with Faraday's input finally compelled the government to act. The Metropolitan Board of Works began construction of a sewage system. A cartoon in *Punch* showed Faraday leaning over the rail of a boat, holding his nose, and offering his business card to Father Thames. It carried the caption "We hope the Dirty Fellow [i.e. Father Thames] will consult the learned Professor."

Before the new system could be completed, the hot summer of 1858 caused widespread sickness and the time became known as "The Great Stink."

Faraday was not finished with suggestions for the public good. In 1830, Captain George Manby had presented a lecture at the Friday Evening Discourses on his plan to build lifesaving stations around the coast of England. Faraday agreed that Manby's plan along with more powerful lighthouses would be beneficial to saving lives. In 1836, Faraday was appointed as Scientific Advisor to Trinity House, an organization charged with providing safe navigation of England's shores.

Faraday investigated methods to improve the strength of lights from lighthouses for Trinity House. The first successful use of Faraday's generator was in 1860 at the Dungeness Lighthouse in the English Channel.

He also inspected lighthouses on a regular basis. At age sixty-nine, he reported on a lighthouse inspection trip, telling of traveling through a snowstorm and finally when trains and carriages could not get through, proceeding by "climbing over hedges, walls, and fields, I succeeded in getting there and making the necessary inquires and observations." He continued to work to increase the efficiency of lighthouses until his retirement from Trinity House in 1865, at age seventy-four.

Faraday continued to have problems with headaches, uncertain memory, and weakness. He noted to the Royal Institution's secretary, "My memory wearies me greatly in working for I cannot remember from day to day the conclusions I come to,

FARADAY GIVING HIS CARD TO FATHER THAMES;

And we hope the Dirty Fellow will consult the learned Professor.

The *Punch* cartoon depicting Faraday's involvement in a campaign to clean up the Thames river. *(Courtesy of Hulton Archive/Getty Images)*

Faraday's method to improve the strength of lights from lighthouses was first implemented at the Dungeness Lighthouse in 1860. *(Courtesy of PCL/Alamy)*

and all has to be thought out many times over. To write it down gives no assistance, for what is written down is itself forgotten."

Still he continued work on a plethora of problems: long distance telegraph, discharge of electricity through gases, properties of chemical suspensions, conservation of paintings at the National Gallery, lighthouse improvements.

He turned again to attempts to convert gravity into electricity. "Surely the force of gravitation and its probable relation to other forms of force may be attacked by experiment."

By dropping objects with wire wrapped around them, he hoped to detect current induced by gravity. All types of metal cores and bricks were tried, but no flicker of the galvanometer occurred. He dropped a 280-pound lead brick from the 165-foot height of the Shot Tower, but no current flowed.

He submitted a paper detailing his experiments and the negative results. At the end he added that he would like to try again for positive results. The paper was submitted to the publication put out by the Royal Institution and was rejected. The editor, George Stokes, asked Faraday to withdraw his paper because the negative results did not lead a person to believe that positive results would ever occur.

Today scientists still have not been able to convert gravity into other forms of force. Electricity, magnetism, and light have all been shown controvertible, but not gravity.

The presidency of the Royal Society was offered to Faraday in 1857. He refused the honor, saying to John Tyndall, "I must remain plain Michael Faraday to the end." Faraday's interest in scientific advances continued. Some time in the late 1850s, Julius Plucker of Bonn visited Faraday's lab. He brought along a new vacuum tube. When electricity was applied to metal electrodes, the gas in the tube showed in a greenish glow. Plucker brought a magnet near the tube, and the discharge flared up in brilliant lights. Faraday remarked, "Oh, to live always in it!"

In 1860, Faraday was again chosen as an elder to the Sandemanian congregation in London.

Faraday's health, both mental and physical, grew more fragile. On October 11, 1861, he told the managers of the Royal Institution,

It is with the deepest feeling that I address you. I entered the Royal Institution in March 1813, nearly forty-nine years ago . . . During that time I have been most happy in your kindness, and in the fostering care which the Royal Institution has bestowed upon me . . . My life has been a happy one and all I desired . . . Still I am not able to do as I have done. I am not competent to perform as I wish . . . I now ask you . . . to accept my resignation of the *Juvenile lectures* . . . I may truly say, that such has been the pleasure of the occupation to me, that my regret must be great than yours need or can be.

He was seventy years old. His duties as director of laboratories continued. Eight months later, he delivered his last Friday Evening Discourse. During the lecture on gas furnaces, Faraday fumbled and scorched his notes. At the end of his presentation, he announced his retirement from those lectures.

In 1858, Queen Victoria at the urging of her husband, Prince Albert, had recognized Faraday's value to England and presented him with a house on the Green at Hampton Court for life. Faraday and Sarah moved into the spacious house in 1862. Faraday immediately considered some improvements. He asked permission from the Board of Works to place fire bricks in three stoves, so that they would not require as much coal. He also requested some of the turf to be removed for a kitchen garden.

While Faraday struggled with his mental health, Sarah's health was also declining. As he wrote to his friend, de la Rive in 1854, "We are both changed, my wife even more than I; for she is indeed very infirm in her limbs, nor have I much expectation that in that respect she will importantly improve."

In 1864, Faraday's friend and later biographer, Dr. Bence Jones, tried to persuade him to accept the presidency of the Royal Institution. Earlier, Faraday had turned down the office

An undated picture of an older Faraday. *(Courtesy of AP Images)*

of president of the Royal Society, but the Royal Institution was even dearer to his heart. He agonized over the decision, as Sarah wrote to Jones, "My poor husband has been so troubled ever since Friday with the thoughts of the *Presidency,* that it has quite affected his health. Part of his difficulty came from the humility valued so highly in the Sandemanian church. How could he be the leader of such an organization and still remain a servant? He insisted that the presidency 'is quite inconsistent with all my life and views.'" Finally, he turned down the honor.

In 1864, his frail health compelled Faraday to resign as an elder from his church. A year later, he also resigned completely from the Royal Institution and turned his Trinity House duties to John Tyndall.

His mind grew weaker as he slid into what he termed, "gentle decay." He was under the care of Dr. Jones, who visited frequently.

Most evenings, he enjoyed sitting in his favorite chair, watching the sunset. Above his bed was a card printed with verses from the biblical book of Psalms, "Remember me, O Lord, with the favour that thou bearest unto thy people: O visit me with thy salvation; That I may see the good of thy chosen, that I may rejoice in the gladness of thy nation, that I may glory with thine inheritance."

As Faraday grew weaker, he spent more time in his chair. On August 25, 1867, he died there. He was just a month short of his seventy-sixth birthday. By his wishes, as he had told his niece, Jane, "I have told several what may be my own desire. To have a plain simple funeral, attended by none but my own relatives, followed by a gravestone of the most ordinary kind, in the simplest earthy place."

His wishes were followed as his relatives buried him at Highgate Cemetery. However, several colleagues came to honor him. A simple headstone marked the grave,

MICHAEL FARADAY
Born 22 September 1791
Died 25 August 1867

Soon after his death, his friend John Tyndall was asked to write about him. He ended his biography with the words, [I] "lay my poor garland on the grave of this Just and faithful knight of God.

Sarah Faraday was cared for by her family and her church after Michael's death, just as he would have wished. He had said, "I must not be afraid; you will be cared for, my wife; you will be cared for." Sarah died in 1879.

Faraday was intrigued by the duality of electricity; possessing both negative and positive properties. However, he also demonstrated a dual personality. He relied on meticulous experiments but also entertained flights of imagination, for example, his ray-vibrations. He showed great humility (as expected by his church) but rose to be one of the world's foremost scientists. His lectures reached men of celebrated status from Prince Albert to famous scientists and also embraced children. He had only rudimentary skills in mathematics, but introduced theories that took eminent mathematicians to explain.

Faraday's legacy is visible everywhere today. His discovered chemicals; carbon tetrachloride and benzene have proven invaluable to the manufacture of dyes, plastics, and medicines. Heat-proof glass dishes are baked in ovens daily.

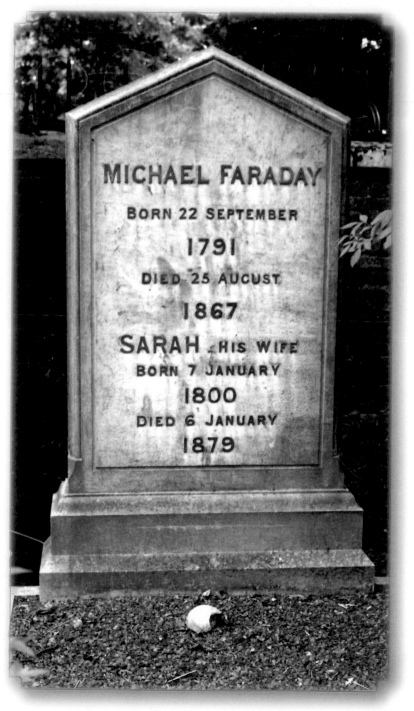

MICHAEL FARADAY

BORN 22 SEPTEMBER

1791

DIED 25 AUGUST

1867

SARAH HIS WIFE

BORN 7 JANUARY

1800

DIED 6 JANUARY

1879

Faraday's simple gravestone

Power plants provide electricity to homes and businesses every day, using Faraday's invention of electromagnetic induction. Electronics depend on the transformer and the capacitor that also came from his experiments. Even the simple motors, such as fans, hair dryers, and CD players owe their start to Faraday.

His influence is immortalized in two units named for him: the farad, measuring capacitance, and the faraday, measuring electrolysis.

The Christmas Juvenile Lectures begun by Faraday continue today, with a series of lectures broadcast by television each year. The Royal Society Michael Faraday Prize was established in 1986. It honors excellence in science communications in the United Kingdom.

Faraday's enthusiasm for science and unending search for knowledge was apparent in his work, and in his many lectures. He was a man who valued more than anything else an open mind, and a willingness to use that mind in the pursuit of greatness, as he made clear in an 1853 lecture:

> Study science with earnestness—search into nature—elicit the truth—reason on it, and reject all which will not stand the closet investigation. Keep your imagination within bounds, taking heed lest it run away with your judgment. Above all, let me warn you young ones of the danger of being led away by the superstitions which at this day of boasted progress are a disgrace to the age, and which afford astonishing proofs of the vast floods of ignorance overwhelming and desolating the highest places.

timeline

1791   Born September 22, 1791, near London.

1805   Starts apprenticeship as bookbinder.

1812   Finishes apprenticeship as bookbinder.

1813   Becomes assistant technician to Sir Humphry Davy at Royal Institution; travels Europe with Davy.

1816   Delivers first lecture at Royal Institution.

1820   Discovers carbon tetrachloride.

1821   Marries Sarah Barnard; discovers principle of electric motor, and electromagnetic rotation.

1823   Elected to the French Academy of Sciences; liquefies chlorine.

1824   Discovers benzene; works on heat-proof glass.

1825   Becomes director of the Royal Institution's laboratory.

1826   Starts Friday Evening Discourses at Royal Institution.

1826   Starts Christmas Juvenile Lectures.

1831   Discovers principle of transformer, principle of dynamo, and electromagnetic induction.

1832   Determines that electricities are the same, regardless of source; investigates oatmeal fraud for Navy; states his laws of electrolysis.

1836   Scientific advisor to Trinity House.

1840   Elected elder of Sandemanian church.

1867   Dies in England at house provided by Queen Victoria on August 25.

Sources

CHAPTER ONE: Blacksmith's son, Bookbinder's Apprentice

p. 16, "Even the lower orders . . ." Alan Hirshfeld, *The Electric Life of Michael Faraday* (New York: Walker & Company, 2006), 6.

p. 16, "intended to promote both Amusement . . ." James Hamilton, *A Life of Discovery: Michael Faraday, Giant of the Scientific Revolution* (New York: Random House, 2002), 401.

p. 18, "had so much *accurate* information . . ." Ibid., 8.

p. 18, "the most wonderful and most . . ." L. Pearce Williams, *Michael Faraday: A Biography* (New York: Basic Books Inc., 1965), 17.

p. 18, "gave me my foundations . . ." Hamilton, *A Life of Discovery*, 8.

p. 20, "the most prominent words . . ." Williams, *Michael Faraday: A Biography*, 16.

p. 23, "Sir, when I first evinced . . ." Hamilton, *A Life of Discovery*, 12.

CHAPTER TWO: Scientific Apprentice

p. 27, "It is evident that in this . . ." Hamilton, *A Life of Discovery*, 25.

p. 27, "The letter required no answer . . ." Williams, *Michael Faraday: A Biography*, 28.

p. 29, "letter writing improves: first . . ." Hamilton, *A Life of Discovery*, 31.

p. 29, "I found myself in the midst . . ." Ibid., 32.

p. 30, "I found that some of the zinc . . ." Hirshfeld, *The Electric Life of Michael Faraday,* 20.

p. 30, "at the first convenient opportunity . . ." Dr. Bence Jones, *The Life and Letters of Faraday* (Philadelphia: J. B. Lippincott and Co., 1870), 1:52.

p. 30, "I must resign philosophy . . ." Ibid.

p. 31, "great zeal, power of memory . . ." Hamilton, *A Life of Discovery,* 38.

p. 31-32, "I have found a person . . ." Ibid., 41.

p. 32, "I have been engaged . . ." Ibid., 45.

p. 33, "What is the longest . . ." Hirshfeld, *The Electric Life of Michael Faraday*, 39.

p. 34, "their attentions are to . . ." Jones, *The Life and Letters of Faraday*, 147.

p. 34, "Davy . . .goes on discovering . . ." Ibid., 195.

p. 34, "he seemed of a dark countenance . . ." Ibid., 46.

p. 36, "only a degenerate idle people . . ." Hirshfeld, *The Electric Life of Michael Faraday*, 53.

p. 36, "We admired Davy, we loved . . ." Ibid.

p. 36, "And now, my dear Sirs . . ." Ibid.

p. 36-37, "She is haughty and proud . . ." Ibid., 54.

CHAPTER THREE: Early Experiments at the Royal Institution

p. 39, "Pray make an investigation . . ." Hirshfeld, *The Electric Life of Michael Faraday,* 58.

p. 40, "I have uniformly received the active . . ." Ibid., 59.

p. 41, "We have subdued this monster," Hamilton, *A Life of Discovery,* 124.

p. 41, "It was the beginning of . . ." Williams, *Michael Faraday: A Biography,* 44.

p. 43, "If M. Davy would be . . ." Hirshfeld, *The Electric Life of Michael Faraday*, 61.

p. 45-46, "His powers, unshackled, range . . ." Ibid., 64.

p. 46, "On Monday evening there is . . ." Jones, *The Life and Letters of Faraday,* 312.

p. 46, "What is the pest . . ." Williams, *Michael Faraday: A Biography,* 96.

p. 47, "I wished for a moment . . ." Hirshfeld, *The Electric Life of Michael Faraday*, 68.

p. 47, "brilliant sparkling ocean, stirred . . ." Hamilton, *A Life of Discovery,* 149.

p. 47, "There will be no bustle . . ." Hirshfeld, *The Electric Life of Michael Faraday*, 70.

p. 47, "On June 12, 1821, he married . . ." Tyndall, *Biography of Michael Faraday,* 38.

p. 48, "Oh, my dear Sarah . . ." Hirshfeld, *The Electric Life of Michael Faraday*, 71.

p. 48, "That is between me . . ." Ibid.

p. 48, "Surely there is a vein . . ." Hamilton, *A Life of Discovery,* 14.

p. 48, "What a treat a visit . . ." Williams, *Michael Faraday: A Biography,* 100.

p. 49, "Cut them in two . . ." Ibid., 101.

p. 49, "Evil is a name . . ." Hamilton, *A Life of Discovery,* 296.

p. 50, "I am very much better . . ." Ibid., 102.

CHAPTER FOUR: Experiments and Rotation

p. 53, "I am naturally skeptical . . ." Hirshfeld, *The Electric Life of Michael Faraday,* 78.

p. 56, "There they go!" Ibid., 80.

p. 56-57, "as they in part affect . . ." Jones, *The Life and Letters of Faraday,* Vol. 1, 339.

p. 57, "I have regretted ever since . . ." Williams, *Michael Faraday: A Biography,* 158.
p. 57, "I am bold enough sir . . ." Hirshfeld, 83.
p. 57, "have been the discoverer . . ." Ibid., 84.
p. 58, "we earnestly recommend . . ." Hamilton, *A Life of Discovery,* 169.
p. 58, "Considering the very subordinate . . ." Hirshfeld, *The Electric Life of Michael Faraday*, 85.
p. 59, "I have no doubt at present . . ." Williams, *Michael Faraday: A Biography,* 125.
p. 59-60, "In solids the matter exerts . . ." Ibid.
p. 60, "I met with another explosion . . ." Hamilton, *A Life of Discovery,* 187.
p. 60,62, "the tube became filled . . ." Williams, *Michael Faraday: A Biography,* 129.
p. 62, "Dear Sir, the oil . . ." Ibid.
p. 64, "Sir H Davy angry . . ." Hirshfeld, *The Electric Life of Michael Faraday*, 86.

CHAPTER FIVE: Lectures
p. 65, "we are having a hard struggle . . ." Hamilton, *A Life of Discovery,* 201.
p. 67, "[We] . . .have established . . ." Ibid., 198.
p. 67, "The most prominent requisite to . . ." Jones, *The Life and Letters of Faraday,* 1: 74.
p. 67-68, "A flame should be lighted . . ." Ibid.
p. 68, "if at a loss for a word . . ." Hirshfeld, *The Electric Life of Michael Faraday,* 99.
p. 68, "A lecturer should appear easy . . ." Ibid.
p. 69, "I am persuaded that all persons . . ." Ibid., 96.
p. 69, "the most rational and pleasurable . . ." Ibid.
p. 70, "I claim the privilege . . ." Michael Faraday, "The Chemical History of a Candle," *Modern History*

Sourcebook, http://www.fordham.edu/halsall/mod/
1860faraday-candle.html, August 1998.

p. 71, "Curiously enough, however, what we . . ." Ibid., 8.

p. 72, "let me hope that none . . ." Ibid., 11.

p. 72, "Now I must take you . . ." Ibid., 39.

p. 72, "We come here to be philosophers." Ibid., 5.

p. 74, "We are not to suppose . . ." Michael Faraday, "Lectures on the Forces of Matter," *Modern History Sourcebook*, http://www.fordham.edu/halsall/mod/1859Faraday-forces. html., August 1998.

p. 74, "Why do I hold the bottle . . ." Ibid., 3.

p. 74, "I want you to observe . . ." Ibid., 23.

p. 75, "Here is a little fragment . . ." Ibid., 27.

p. 75, "Philosophers have been suspecting . . ." Ibid., 32.

p. 75, "He made us all laugh . . ." Hirshfeld, *The Electric Life of Michael Faraday*, 103.

p. 75, "At the end of the lectures . . ." Ibid., 104.

p. 76, "The [Royal] Institution has been . . ." Ibid., 111.

CHAPTER SIX: The Discovery of Electromagnetism

p. 77, "This is exceedingly beautiful . . ." Hamilton, *A Life of Discovery*, 235.

p. 77-78, "98. Mercury on tin plate . . ." Ibid., 237.

p. 78, "they may serve to indicate . . ." Ibid.

p. 81, "oscillated and settled at last . . ." Ibid., 246.

p. 81-82, "I am busy just now . . ." Jones, *The Life and Letters of Faraday*, 2:3.

p. 82, "Hence here distinct conversion . . ." Ibid., 4.

p. 85, "I know not, but I wager . . ." Hirshfeld, *The Electric Life of Michael Faraday,* 123.

p. 86, "I have rather . . . been desirous . . ." Ibid., 124.

p. 86, "It is quite comfortable to me . . ." Jones, *The Life and Letters of Faraday,* 2:10.

p. 86-87, "I never took more pains . . ." Hirshfeld, *The Electric Life of Michael Faraday,* 126.

p. 87, "To render you complete justice . . ." Ibid., 127.

CHAPTER SEVEN: Faraday's Laws

p. 89, "physicist is both to my mouth . . ." Hamilton, *A Life of Discovery,* 261.

p. 92, "Those bodies which, being interposed . . ." Michael Faraday, *Experimental Researches in Electricity* (Mineola, New York: Dover Publications, Inc., 2004), 165.

p. 92, "That *for a constant quantity* . . ." Ibid., 65.

p. 95, "I went into the cube . . ." Hirshfeld, *The Electric Life of Michael Faraday,* 142.

p. 96, "Faraday figured their particles . . ." Tyndall, *Biography of Michael Faraday,* 18.

p. 97, "Gravity . . .will not turn a corner . . ." Ibid., 17.

p. 98, "The science of electricity . . ." Hirshfeld, *The Electric Life of Michael Faraday,* 144.

p. 98, "I am unfortunate in a want . . ." Ibid., 145.

p. 100, "I have far more confidence . . ." Ibid.

p. 100, "memory [was] so treacherous . . ." Ibid., 151.

p. 100, "your Uncle is pretty well . . ." Hamilton, *A Life of Discovery,* 295.

p. 100-101, "enjoys the country exceedingly . . ." Hirshfeld, *The Electric Life of Michael Faraday,* 152.

p. 101, "in far better condition . . ." Hamilton, *A Life of Discovery,* 300.

p. 101, " . . .she is very patient . . ." Ibid., 304.

p. 102, "low in health and spirits . . ." Geoffrey Cantor, *Michael Faraday: Sandemanian and Scientist* (New York: St. Martin's Press, 1991), 63.

p. 102, "God has been pleased . . ." Ibid., 202.

p. 104, "How wonderful it is . . ." Ibid.

CHAPTER EIGHT: Lines of Force

p. 105, "I have long been *vowed* . . ." Hamilton, *A Life of Discovery,* 313.

p. 105-106, "a labourer of many years . . ." Ibid.

p. 107, "I would not miss . . ." Ibid., 317.

p. 108, " . . .for if space be an . . ." Williams, *Michael Faraday: A Biography,* 377.

p. 108, "All our perception and . . ." Hirshfeld, *The Electric Life of Michael Faraday,* 162.

p. 108, "The powers around the centres . . ." Ibid., 163.

p. 110, "inoculated with Faraday fire . . ." Ibid., 155.

p. 111, "no effect"; "still no effect . . ." Ibid., 157.

p. 111, "This fact will most likely . . ." Ibid., 158.

p. 111, "effect was good"; "very fine . . ." Ibid.

p. 112, "All the views which Faraday . . ." Ibid., 165.

p. 112, "one of the most singular . . ." Tyndall, *Biography of Michael Faraday,* 32.

p. 112, "The view which I am . . ." Hirshfeld, *The Electric Life of Michael Faraday,* 167.

p. 113, "From first to last, understand . . ." Ibid.

p. 113, "The propagation of light . . ." Ibid.

p. 113, "What's the go . . ." Ibid., 175.

p. 113, "But what is the *particular . . .*" Ibid.

p. 114-115, "The method which Faraday . . ." Ibid., 185.

p. 115, "Every student therefore should . . ." Ibid., 182.

p. 115, "I was at first . . ." Ibid., 184.

p. 115, "First—the quickness . . ." Ibid., 186.

p. 116, "weave a web across . . ." Ibid.

p. 116, "Ho, Maxwell, cannot . . ." Ibid., 188.

p. 116, "The electromagnetic theory of light . . ." Ibid., 189.

p. 117, "If by anything I have written . . ." Ibid., 193.

p. 119, "I think the system of education . . ." Hamilton, 354.

CHAPTER NINE: Legacy

p. 120, "before they had sunk . . ." Hamilton, *A Life of Discovery,* 383.

p. 120, "If we neglect this subject . . ." Ibid., 384.

p. 121, "We hope the Dirty Fellow . . ." Ibid.

p. 121, "climbing over hedges, walls . . ." Hirshfeld, *The Electric Life of Michael Faraday,* 206.

p. 121-122, "My memory wearies me greatly . . ." Ibid., 204.

p. 123, "Surely the force of gravitation . . ." Ibid., 205.

p. 124, "I must remain plain Michael . . ." Tyndall,

p. 124, "Oh, to live always . . ." Hirshfeld, *The Electric Life of Michael Faraday,* 212.

p. 125, "It is with the deepest feeling . . ." Williams, *Michael Faraday: A Biography,* 497.

p. 125, "We are both changed . . ." Hamilton, *A Life of Discovery,* 386.

p. 127, "My poor husband has been . . ." Cantor, *Michael Faraday: Sandemanian and Scientist,* 279.

p. 127, "Remember me, O Lord, . . ." Hamilton, *A Life of Discovery,* 393.

p. 127, "I have told several . . ." Ibid., 394.

p. 128, "lay my garland . . ." Tyndall, *Biography of Michael Faraday,* 43.

p. 128, "I must not be afraid . . ." Hamilton, *A Life of Discovery,* 398.

p. 130, "Study science with earnestness . . ." Hirshfeld. *The Electric Life of Michael Faraday,* 199.

Bibliography

Cantor, Geoffrey. *Michael Faraday: Sandemanian and Scientist.* New York: St. Martin's Press, 1991.

Faraday, Michael. "The Chemical History of a Candle." *Modern History Sourcebook.* http://www.fordham.edu/halsall/mod/1860faraday-candle.html, August 1998.

_____. *Experimental Researches in Electricity.* Mineola, New York: Dover Publications, Inc., 2004.

_____. "Lectures on the Forces of Matter." *Modern History Sourcebook*, http://www.fordham.edu/halsall/mod/1859Faraday-forces.html, August 1998.

Hamilton, James. *A Life of Discovery: Michael Faraday, Giant of the Scientific Revolution.* New York: Random House, 2002.

Hirshfeld, Alan. *The Electric Life of Michael Faraday.* New York: Walker & Company, 2006.

Jones, Bence. *The Life and Letters of Faraday.* Philadelphia: J. B. Lippincott and Co., 1870.

Williams, L. Pearce. *Michael Faraday: A Biography.* New York: Basic Books Inc., 1965.

Web sites

http://www.gutenberg.org/etext/14474 and http://www.gutenberg.org/etext/14986
The complete text of "Experimental Researches in Electricity, Volume 1" and "The Chemical History of A Candle" are available to download from this Web site.

http://www.rigb.org/./registrationControl?action=home
The official Web site of the Royal Institution of Great Britain.

http://physics.about.com/od/electromagnetics/Electromagnetics.htm
A number of articles about electromagnetics.

http://www.archive.org/details/lettersoffaraday00fararich
Visitors to this Web site may download the text of Faraday's correspondence with Schoenbien.

http://www.wvic.com/how-gen-works.htm
A graphic and text explaining how an electric generator, similar to one created by Michael Faraday, works.

Index